Wine making and lean manufacturing; all a wine maker needs to know

INTRODUCTION

How different thinking and methods can boost your business

How do you define and evaluate 'success'? Win a reward at school and in career, gaining a high score in an exam, study and graduate from a school with reputation, having cheerful families and friends, having a lots of money and or be a wonderful person? Life is about Plan, Leaning, execution, action, exploring and go on.

There is no absolute right or wrong or certain answer to a question.

Key word tag: lean, six sigma, JIT, Kaizen, 8 waste, 5S, standardization, Jidoka, respect, methodology, process, strategies, priority, stability, customer relation, winery, etc.

What is lean

Lean come from Toyota executive who was the most ferocious foe of waste human history has produced, identified the first seven types of wastes which now is eight.

Lean refers to reducing waste in your business. Waste is anything that doesn't benefit your bottom line or add value to your organization.

Lean Six Sigma: 8 Wastes

Talent

Underutilizing
people's talents,
skills, & knowledge.

Inventory

Excess products
and materials not
being processed.

Motion

Unnecessary
movements by
people (e.g., walking).

Waiting

Wasted time waiting
for the next step
in a process.

Transportation

Unnecessary
movements of
products & materials.

Defects

Efforts caused by
rework, scrap, and
incorrect information.

Overproduction

Production that is
more than needed or
before it is needed.

Overprocessing

More work or higher
quality than is required
by the customer.

Waste Root causes and result impact

1. Defects

Defects are one of the most visible examples of waste and can be easy to grasp in any industry. Defects refer to any product or service that doesn't meet commercial specifications and must be discarded, or fixed via additional resources.

Defects can cause waste in numerous ways in addition to the capital used to scrap or rebuild a product or service. Defects will affect delivery times, logistics, and ultimately customer satisfaction. Your business should not spend an extra second on the rescheduling, paperwork and critical thinking that goes into fixing defects.

2. Overproduction

Overproduction occurs when you produce more product that is required by your customers. Companies tend to make the mistake of producing a product in large batches. This may seem like a good idea on paper, but market forces change and consumer needs change over time. It's akin to putting all of your eggs in one basket and hoping for the best.

Overproduction leads to excess inventory, which then leads to additional expenditure on storage space and preservation. This does not add value.

3. Waiting

Nobody likes waiting. We've all experienced waiting to be served in a grocery store or having to sit on hold waiting for a contact centre. In a nutshell, waiting is the time it takes to begin another process after finishing one. The time spent waiting between processes and transactions will result in dissatisfied customers.

4. Non-utilized talent

Under-utilizing employees' talents, skills and knowledge can have a detrimental effect on an organization. There are innumerous benefits to recognizing the value of skills and ideas that improve a process, especially from employees on the frontline that see process waste on a daily basis. A few examples include; a lack of teamwork, limited training, poor communication, duplicated administrative tasks and much more. Employee engagement, not micromanagement, is key to finding out how you can fix waste in your company.

5. Transportation

Transportation waste involves the unnecessary movement of product or information that doesn't add value. This comes in the form of moving a process from one individual to another, within the same department, and to another department. All of this adds unnecessary time onto a process. To eliminate this kind of waste, you can combine tasks and roles, and in extreme cases, reorganize workspaces to reduce physical movement.

6. Inventory

Inventory waste occurs when a product or material is waiting to be sold. This is often the result of:

- Poor monitoring systems
- Misunderstood customer needs
- Unreliable supplier

The difference between inventory waste and overproduction waste is that inventory waste is the value that is being held at a cost. Unlike overproduction, which assumed supplies exceed demand, inventory is material or product that has value but is not moving fast enough to meet customer demand.

7. Motion

Motion is any process that takes up time or capital by employees or machines, that fails to add value to the product being sold. The difference between motion and transportation waste is that motion waste is employee-centric and opposed to product-centric.

Common reasons this occurs include:

- Poor process design and controls
- Poor workstation/shop layout
- Shared tools and machines
- Workstation congestion
- Isolated and siloed operations

- Lack of standard

8. Extra processing

Extra processing involves performing work on a product that does not conform to the customers' expectations. This can occur when a company doesn't have a firm grasp on customer requirements. This should not be confused with "going the extra mile" which does in fact value to a product or service as it can lead to additional commercial interest.

An example of extra processing can include duplicated or replicated data, overdesigned equipment's, multiple signatures and more. This often occurs due to the creation of multiple versions of the same task, process more than is required or long-winded poorly designed processes. Examples include:

- Excessive reports
- Multiple signatures
- Re-entering data and duplicated data
- Lack of standards

Lean Production House framework

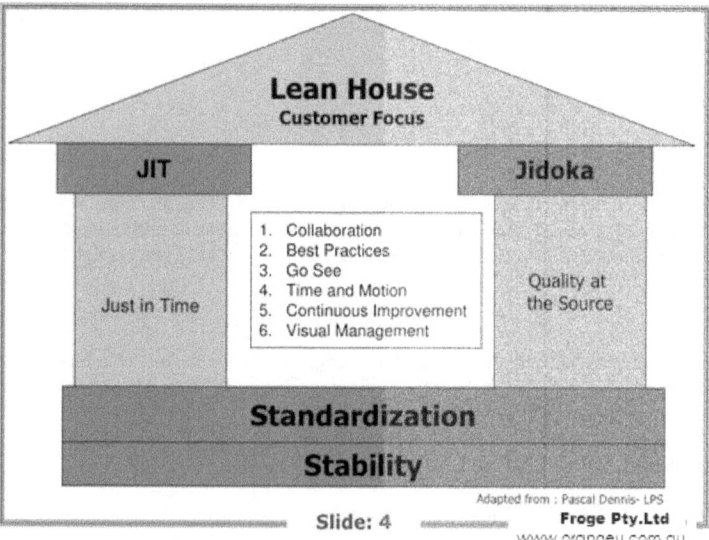

Operational Stability

Leveling

Leveling demand (Heijunka) is defined as the distribution of production valume and mix evenly over time. This will represent the single point schedule in the value stream, in this case at the finished good level.

Standard work

Defines the content, sequence, and timing of work. The goal for standard work: defining the content, sequence, and timing of work to achieve an optimum process for manufacturing product. Stardard work is a key element that is often ignored during Lean implementations. Standard work has been compared to the printed feet in a Arthur Murry dance class.

Henry Ford said: "To standardize a method is to choose out of the many method the best one, and use it. Standardization means nothing unless it means standardizing upward. Today's standardization, instead of being a barricade against improvement, is the necessary foundation on which tomorrow's improvement will be based. If you think of "standardization" as the best that you know today, but which is to be improved tomorrow- you get somewhere. But if you think of standards as confining, then process stops." With this though in mind, it is obvious that standard work is one of the cornerstones of continuous improvement.

Kaizen

Continuous improvement of an entire value stream or an individual process to create more value with less waste.

There are two levels of Kaizen:

- System of flow kaizen focusing on the overall value stream. This is kaizen for management.
- Process kaizen focusing on individual processes. This is kaizen for work teams and team leaders.

JIT: Just in Time Production

A system of production that makes and delivers just what is needed, just when it is needed, and just in the amount needed. JIT and jidoka are the two pillars of the Toyota Production System. JIT relies on Heijunka as a foundation and is comprised of three operating elements: the pull system, takt time, and continuous flow.

Takt time refers to the pace at which the customer is buying products, Takts time is one of the keys to determing how much labour and machine resources are required in the value stream.

One piece flow is the production method that has the least amount of waste, so this is the method that is the goal of lean.

If one-piece flow cannot be achieved, then pull is used. At its simplest, pull can be thought of as simply replacing what has just been used. It is a way to have the value stream produce what the customer has just purchased, meaning that the value stream begins to operate in a make-to-order fashion.

Technical

- Stability
- JIT
- Jidoka
- Kaizen
- Heijunka

Management

- True North
- Tools to focus management attention
- Go and see
- Problem – solving
- Presentation skills
- Project management
- Supportive culture

Philosophy/basic thinking

- Customer first
- People are most important asset
- Kaizen
- Go and see   Focus on Floor
- Efficiency thinking

Lean planning and Control Chart

Lean wants to first create product families that can hen become value streams, A product family is a set of parts that go through roughly the same processes. Value stream mapping is done for each product family, and determines how the value stream will operate, as well as providing a list of kaizen improvement activities that will need to worked on to achieve the future state.

LEAN SUPPLY CHAIN MANAGEMENT ESSENTIALS

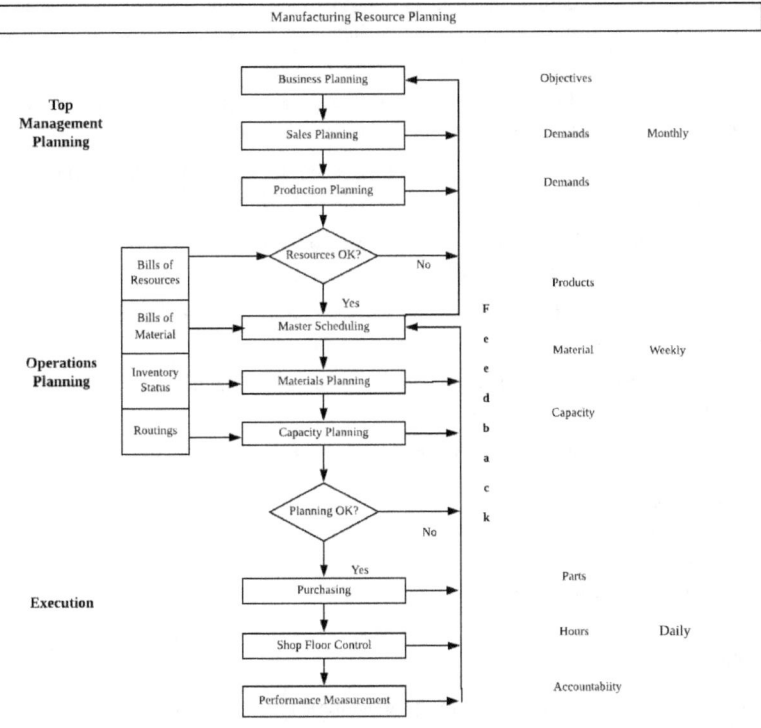

Sales and operations planning is the same as it is traditionally, with the same objectives and processes.

Buffering strategy determines how work into the value stream will be leveled, one of the seven principles of a Lean value stream.

The production rate: Takt time comes from the production rate determined in the sales and operation plan. This rate becomes the heartbeat of the value stream and determines how fast product should be produced.

Demand leveling is the execution of the buffering strategy, and is often called heijunka. This demand leveling occurs at the pace maker operation, which is the operation where flow to the customers begins.

The heijunka plan creates demand for all of the other processes in the value stream and can be obtained by a simple gross explosion of the heijunka plan through the bill of materials.

Standard work refers to defining the content, sequence, and timing of work to achieve an optimum process for manufacturing product. Standard work has been compared to the dance steps in an Arthur Murray dance class.

The operator balance chart determines how many people are required to perform the work required at the takt rate, and is the first part of the capacity plan.

Machine intervals determine how large the lot size needs to be to perform the runtime, and setup times required to produce at the takt time. This is the second input to the capacity plan.

The capacity plan contains the work time, effective work time, number of people, machine shifts, and intervals for the machines and the takt time.

The pull system is planned using the demand explosion from the heijunka schedule, then executes replenishement based on part usage.

Kaizen management is the philosophy of continuous improvement in action through project management and on-the-floor activity.

A few areas lean planning and hierarchy differs significantly from traditional one:

- Leveling production
- Pull systems
- Flow
- Interval to determine lot size

Leveling Production

Leveling production is one of the main ways to address mura, one of the three main classification of waste.

- The key concept is to make the same products in the same quantities in the same timeframes on a repetitive basis.
- Once in a while, say monthly or quarterly, the mix of production is reviewed and adjusted to meet the actual demand.

Eliminating the variation of different products and varing quantities in production reduces lots of other wastes. This doesn't mean that all products are built in the exact same quantity, but that each product has a production quantity that doesn't vary from build cycle to build cycle.

Pull Systems

In production

- the production of items only as demanded for use or to replace those taken for use.

- In material control, the withdrawal of inventory as demanded by the using operations. Material is not issued until a signal comes from the user.
- The new logic says that when a part is used, you make it and put it back in stock.

Benefits of a Kanban pull system

- **More capital** – less money will be invested in storage space for inventory
- **Increased market dynamism** – Whether it is market forces that affect scalability or an aspect of the product itself, it can be damaging to have inventory consisting of un-sellable products.
  Less work in progress (WIP)
- **Improved production environment** – Kanban provides visual clarity and can promote objective and rational discussion among team members
- **Easy monitoring** – All team members will have a constant feedback of performance via a breakdown of every stage from start to finish.

Flow

The more f low you can design into the value stream, the shorter the lead time will be and the less waste there will be. Flow, not pull, is the main objective of lean production. Flow takes the form of either one-piece flow or first in first out flow. Keeping the material moving is one of the primary objectives when designing the value stream. Flow in either form will have less waste than a pull system, because flow will only contain items that have been sold and scheduled, while the pull system will need to have some of all the parts that can possibly be needed, so flow will have less waste than pull. Creating flow eliminate levels in the bill of materials(BOM). As we eliminate the need to stock parts, we can eliminate the BOM levels necessary to keep track of this inventory.

Interval as Lot Size

The interval can be thought of as equivalent of the period order quantity lot size, but ti is much more integral to the lean planning process than lot sizing in a traditional system.

- Interval drives set up reduction activity as well as crap and rework reduction activity.
- The more available capacity, the smaller the lot sizes can be.

Pull Production

A method of production control in which downstream activities signal their needs to upstream activities. Pull production strives to eliminate overproduction and is one of the three major components of a complete just-in-time production system.

Jidoka

Jidoka is a composite term meaning manual or automatic line stop. Many jidoka stories revolve around the ability of the oprators to stop the line any time a problem is encountered.

The elements of jidoka include:

- Separate operator and machine activities
- Mistake-proofing
- In-station process control

Jidoka includes self-stop as well as mistake-proofing, single-minute exchange of die, visual controls, 6 sigma/SPC(Statistical Process Control), separating human and machine work, 5S, etc

Jidoka means thatv a machine safely stops when the normal processing is completed. It also means that should a quality or equipment problem arise, the machine detects the problem on its own and stops, preventing defective products from being produced. As a result, only products satisfying the quality standards will be passed on to the next processes on the production line. "Since a machine automatically stops when processing is completed or when a problem arises and is communicated via the 'andon', operators can confidently continue performing work at another machines, as well as easily identify the problem cause and prevent its recurrence, This means that each operator can be in charge of many machines, resulting in higher productivity, while the continuous improvement lead to greater processing capacity". From toyota

Improvement and respect

- Culture of continuous improvement
- Respect for people
  -Morale results from employees having a voice and driving improvement.
  - Safety Improvement is never made at t he risk of poor safety. The point on safety goes back to the people-focused culture that must be developed for lean to be most effective. While we don't think that any company is intentionally ignoring safety issues, the emphasis on safety first is an important one. How is the morale at your company? Why do you think it is that way? What can be done to improve it?
  - Community imvolvement. A company must be more than a place for shareholders to make money. It needs to be part of a community., from the aspects of both providing meaningful employment to the citizens of the community and being a good corporate citizen. The company and its employees must actively participate in the activities of the community.

5 S

5S is a five-step methodology aimed at creating and maintaining an organized visual workplace for continued process improvement and efficiency.

This is a very practical system aids for analyzing the current organizational space and removing what isn't necessary.

- **Sorting out** – This step entails going through all of your work tools and materials to determine what is needed and what isn't. To find the value of each item, ask yourself:

  - **What** is the purpose of this item?
  - **Why** is it here?
  - **How** often is it used?
  - **Who** uses it?

If can't find useful answers to these questions? You probably don't need it.

- **Set in order** – Once the unnecessary clutter has gone, you can rearrange the workspace to align with the goals and immediate requests of your team.
- **Sweep** – Create a plan for regular maintenance and cleaning for tools and equipment
- **Standardise** – Turn one time efforts into habits. Whether if its an online checklist or verbal reminders, set aside time to help foster an environment where tasks become routine.

- **Sustain** – Ensure long-term sustainability. Whether you're a manager or new starter, everyone needs to be on board with the new program. This is why documenting procedures and ensuring they are easy to find is so important for process improvement.

LEAN management executive learning rules

Rule 1: Flow on a MICRO- OR Macro-scale is achieved only when self-interest is satisfied or removed.

Rule 2: "Respect for people" principle is required, not optional.

Rule 3: KAIZEN is the principle learning process.

Rule 4: Effort must be continuous – practice everyday

Rule 5: Application must be broad-based; no person or department is exempt rom learning and participation.

Rule 6: All managers must have cross- functional work-experiences

Rule 7: Thinking and doing must be balanced.

Rule 8: Question everything – ask "why?"

Rule 9: Spend ideas, not dollars

Rule 10: Make Most changes rapidly

Rule 11: Ready, study and try new things

Rule 12: Have fun

What is 6 Sigma

A comprehensive and flexible system for achieving, sustaining and maximizing business success. Six sigma is uniquely driven by close understanding of customer needs, disciplined use of facts, data and statistical analysis, and diligent attention to managing, improving, and reinventing business processes.

The Business Success you may achieve are broad because the proven benefits of six sigma system are diverse, including

- Cost reduction
- Productivity improvement
- Market-share growth
- Customer retention
- Cycle-time reduction
- Culture change

- Product/service development

  And more

Clarifying 'Service' and 'manufacturing'

"Service" processes and businesses. When throughout this chapter we talk about "Services" or "service and support" processes, what we mean is any part of company not directly involved in designing or producing tangible products. That can mean sales, finance, marketing, procurements, customer support, logistics, or human resources and more in any organization, transactional, commercial, nontechnical, support and administrative.

"Manufacturing" processes. By manufacturing we mean only those activities relating to the development and production of tragible products. Other terms used to describe these are "plant floor","productioin", sometimes "engineering" and "product development".

Making Six Sigma work in services

Tip#1 Start with the process

Have you ever go to a dance or party where at the end, someone turns up the lights? It's usually a bit of a shock, maybe a litter sad, but also gives you a chance to see things more clearly.

In most Service organizations, starting to investigate processes is like turning up the lights. Though often something of a rude awakening, it also can be an enlightening event that gets the 6 sigma effort off to a fast start. As people discover what's really going on, they can recognize that one party seems to be over but that another one is getting under way.

Tip#2 Fine-tune the problem

When the bright lights come on, it takes a few seconds for your eyes to adjust. It takes a while for a group to see and understand the issues around them as clearly as they should. That's to be expected ,and the only way to get a really clear perspective is to get to work detailing your processes and customer requirements, and the issues affecting them. In the meantime, though, fuzzy vision and an over- eagerness to " straighten this place up" can lead to projects and improvement initiatives that aren't well defined.

Tip#3 Make good use of Facts and Data to reduce ambiguity

One of the biggest abstacles between you and clarifying issues, measuring performances, and generating improvement in the Service arena is the fact that things often are not well described or defined.

Tip#4 Don't overemphasize Statistics

This will be the most controversial of suggestions.

It is most important to Six Sigma improvement that people in Services or Manufacturing learn to ask critical questions about their process and customers:

- How do we really know that?
- How to test our assumptions?
- What are the data telling us?
- Is there better way to do this?

Six Sigma Road Map

Step one:Identify Core processes and key Customers
Step two: Define Customer requirements
Step Three: Measure Current Performance
Step Four: Prioritize, analyze and implement improvement
Step Five: Expand and integrate the six sigma system

The Key to successful improvement: selecting the right six sigma projects
Executive leadership training
Launching a reasonable number of projects
"Scope" Projects Properly
Focus on Both Efficiency and Customer Benefits

Steps towards Effective Project Selection
Good project selection is itself a process; if you follow it well, you can improve your hit rate substantially.
Below are some key questions and steps that will help drive the project selection process. The assumption here is that projects are being chosen by a group, usually of senior managers. But even if you're choosing projects on your own for organization, the same consideration apply.
Choosing Sources for project ideas
As is true of any process, input are key to an effective result.
If you take into consideration only a few anecdotal piece of data as you decide where to focus your Six Sigma efforts, you are that much more likely to have irrelevant or unmanageable projects.
External Sources. These fall into three categories: Voice of the customer; Voice of the market; and comparison with competitors.
Internal Sources. These inputs help you to identify challenges that your business faces in defining and /or achieving its market and customer strategies. Questions they should help you answer include these:
What are the barriers between us and our strategic goals?

What new acquisitions need to be integrated so that they are profitable and aligned with our desired market images?
What new products, services, locations, or other capabilities do we hope to launch, to better provide value to customers and shareholders?
Internal sources. The frustrations, issues, problems, and opportunities visible inside your operations are the third key source of possible six sigma projects. "Voice of the process" and "Voice of employee"

What major delays slow down our processes? Where is there a high volume of defects and or rework? Where are the cost of poor quality increasing? What concerns or ideas have employees or managers raised?

Defining Criteria for project selection

1. Results or business benefits criteria
   Impact on external customers and requirements. How beneficial or important is this problem or opportunity to our "paying customers" or key external audiences (eg, shareholders, regulators, supply-chain partners)?
   Impact on business strategy, competitive postion. What value will this potential project have in helping us to realize our business vision, implement our market strategy, or improve our competitive postion?
   Impact on "Core competencies" How will this possible six sigma project affect our mix and capabilities in "core competencies"?Could involve strengthening a core competency, or "off-loading" an activity no longer deemed a key internal skill.
   Financial impact (eg. Cost reduction, improved efficiency, increased sales, market-share gain) what is the short-term dollar gain likely to be? Long-term? How accurately can we project these numbers?(Beware of inflating gains beyond what's realistic)
   Urgency What kind of lead time do we have to address this issue or capitalize on this opportunity.
   Trend. Is this problem, issue, or opportunity getting bigger or smaller over time? What will happen if we do nothing?
   Sequence or Dependency. Are other possible projects or opportunities dependent on dealing with this issue firs?
2. Feasibility Criteria
   Resources needed. How many people, how much time, how much money Is this project likely to need?
   Expertise available. What knowledge or technical skills will be needed for this projects? Do we have them available and accessible?
   Complexity. How complicated or difficulty do we anticipate it will be to develop the improvement solution? To implement it?
   Likelihood of success. In reasonable timeframe.

Support or buy-in. How much support for this project can wen anticipate from key groups within the organization? Will we be able to make a good case for doing this project?

3. Organizational Impact Criteria

Learning benefits. What new knowledge- might we gain from projects? Cross-functional benefits. To what extent will this project help to break down barriers between groups and create better whole process management?

Selecting project "Dos and Don't's"

Do- Base your improvement Project selection on solid criteria.

Balance results, feasibility, and organizational impact issues. Good project selection can be a key to early success.

Do- Balance efficiency/ cost-cutting with external-focused, customer value projects

The customer focus theme is a source of Six Sigma's Strength. Putting your energies into short-term savings only sends the wrong signal and reduces your chance of boosting customer satisfaction and loyalty.

Do- Prepare for an effective "handoff" to the improvement team.

A technique like the project rationale can give a good start to a project by defining clear issues and objectives.

Don't – Choose too many projects.

Improvement takes care and feeding on the part of leaders and experts, especially at the beginning. It's tempting to overextend your resources and capabilities.

Don't- Create world hunger project

Even more common than "too many" is "too big". Better to get a too small project done more quickly- as long as results are meaningful- than to have a too-big project drag on for months.

Don't- Fail to explain the reasoning for the projects chosen.

Everyone has problems they think should be top- priority. Ensuring support for the ones you choose means providing a good rationale for your priorities.

DMAIC model

Define, Measure, Analyze, Improve, Control- with Some variation

Based on "Plan-Do-Check-Act" cycle

Potential Advantages of DMAIC

1. Making a fresh start
2. Giving a new context to familiar tools
3. Creating a consistent approach.
4. Putting a priority on "Customer" and "measurement"
5. Offering both "process improvement" and "Process design" paths to improvement

Industry 4.0

Industry 4.0 is a name given to the current trend of automation and data exchange in manufacturing technologies. It includes cyber-physical systems, the Internet of things,cloud computing and cognitive computing. Industry 4.0 is commonly referred to as the fourth industrial revolution.

Industry 4.0 fosters what has been called a "smart factory". Within modular structured smart factories, cyber-physical systems monitor physical processes, create a virtual copy of the physical world and make decentralized decisions. Over the Internet of Things, cyber-physical systems communicate and cooperate with each other and with humans in real-time both internally and across organizational services offered and used by participants of the value chain.

Industry 4.0 - Technological pillars

Wine is an alcoholic drink made from fermented grapes. Yeast consumes the sugar in the grapes and converts it to ethanol, carbon dioxide, and heat. Different varieties of grapes and strains of yeasts produce different styles of wine. These variations result from the complex interactions between the biochemical development of the grape, the reactions involved in fermentation, the terroir, and the production process. Many countries enact legal appellations intended to define styles and qualities of wine. These typically restrict the geographical origin and permitted varieties of grapes, as well as other aspects of wine production. Wines not made from grapes include rice wine and fruit wines such as plum, cherry, pomegranate, currant and elderberry. The wine maker is someone that has the job of ripening healthy grapes in the vineyard, full of grape sugar that can by the action of yeast, be fermented into alcohol. If the grape sugar is fermented, the wine will be dry, and enlivened by the acidity that is naturally present in grapes. The more grape sugar fermented into alcohol, the more potent the wine will be. Wines can vary from less than 8% to more than 15% alcohol, with 13.5% being the average.

The major characteristics that sets wine apart from other drinks is the ability of the best wines to last for decades and sometimes centuries and improving as time goes by. Nothing else consumed is capable of remaining healthy, thrilling and alive over such a long period of time.

Historical background

Wine has been produced for thousands of years. The earliest known traces of wine are from Georgia (c. 6000 BC), Iran (c. 5000 BC), and Sicily (c. 4000 BC) although there is evidence of a similar alcoholic drink being consumed earlier in China (c. 7000 BC). The earliest known winery is the 6,100-year-old Areni-1 winery in Armenia. Wine reached the Balkans by 4500 BC and was consumed and celebrated in ancient Greece, Thrace and Rome. Throughout history, wine has been consumed for its intoxicating effects.

Wine has long played an important role in religion. Red wine was associated with blood by the ancient Egyptians and was used by both the Greek cult of Dionysus and the Romans in their Bacchanalia; Judaism also incorporates it in the Kiddush and Christianity in the celebration of the Eucharist.

The earliest archaeological and archaeo-botanical evidence for grape wine and viniculture, dating to 6000–5800 BC was found on the territory of modern Georgia. Both archaeological and genetic evidence suggest that the earliest production of wine elsewhere was relatively later, likely having taken place in the Southern Caucasus (which encompasses Armenia, Georgia and Azerbaijan), or the West Asian region between Eastern Turkey, and northern Iran.

A 2003 report by archaeologists indicates a possibility that grapes were mixed with rice to produce mixed fermented drinks in China in the early years of the seventh millennium BC. Pottery jars from the Neolithic site of Jiahu, Henan, contained traces of tartaric acid and other organic compounds commonly found in wine. However, other fruits indigenous to the region, such as hawthorn, cannot be ruled out. If these drinks, which seem to be the precursors of rice wine, included grapes rather than other fruits, they would have been any of the several dozen indigenous wild species in China, rather than Vitis vinifera, which was introduced there 6000 years later.

The spread of wine culture westwards was most probably due to the Phoenicians who spread outward from a base of city-states along the Mediterranean coast of what are today Syria, Lebanon, Israel, and Palestine. The wines of Byblos were exported to Egypt during the Old Kingdom and then throughout the Mediterranean. Evidence includes two Phoenician shipwrecks from 750 BC discovered by Robert Ballard, whose cargo of wine was still intact. As the first great traders in wine (cherem), the Phoenicians seem to have protected it from oxidation with a layer of olive oil, followed by a seal of pinewood and resin, similar to retsina. Although the nuragic Sardinians already consumed wine before the arrival of the Phoenicians.

The earliest remains of Apadana Palace in Persepolis dating back to 515 BC include carvings depicting soldiers from Achaemenid Empire subject nations bringing gifts to the Achaemenid king, among them Armenians bringing their famous wine.

Literary references to wine are abundant in Homer (8th century BC, but possibly relating earlier compositions), Alkman (7th century BC), and others. In ancient Egypt, six of 36 wine amphoras were found in the tomb of King Tutankhamun bearing the name "Kha'y", a royal chief vintner. Five of these amphoras were designated as originating from the king's personal estate, with the sixth from the estate of the royal house of Aten. Traces of wine have also been found in central Asian Xinjiang in modern-day China, dating from the second and first millennia BC.

The first known mention of grape-based wines in India is from the late 4th-century BC writings of Chanakya, the chief minister of Emperor Chandragupta Maurya. In his writings, Chanakya condemns the use of alcohol while chronicling the emperor and his court's frequent indulgence of a style of wine known as madhu.

The ancient Romans planted vineyards near garrison towns so wine could be produced locally rather than shipped over long distances. Some of these areas are now world-renowned for wine production. The Romans discovered that burning sulfur candles inside empty wine vessels kept them fresh and free from a vinegar smell. In medieval Europe, the Roman Catholic Church supported wine because the clergy required it for the Mass. Monks in France made wine for years, aging it in caves. An old English recipe that survived in various forms until the 19th century calls for refining white wine from bastard—bad or tainted bastardo wine.

It is important to note that the history of wines is not its only important criteria. Geography is absolutely crucial. Wine is one of the very few things one can pluck off a shelf and know precisely, which spot on the globe was responsible for it.

Geography as a factor for determining wine characteristics

As earlier stated, geography is crucial in predicting how a particular wine would taste or look like. There are five main factors that influence the geography of a place and these factors in turn indirectly affects the wine produced.

Seasonal Growing Temperature

From the moment the fruit blossoms burst, to the day of the harvest, the grapes are in a race to ripen, and average temperature is one factor that determines when and if they'll cross the finish line. Grapes ripen at different speeds, which means that average temperature is a huge component in terms of determining which varieties should be planted in each region. Pinot Noir and Chardonnay are some of the first grapes to be harvested and grow best with an average temperature of between approximately 57 and 63°F. Zinfandel, on the other hand, is a grape that needs more heat (closer to 64-69°F).

In general, warmer climates allow grapes to fully ripen and mature, developing deep pigments, bold fruit flavors, greater sweetness, and higher alcohol content. On the flip side, cooler climates show a softer side, accentuating white wines' minerality, maintaining juicy acidity, and ensuring a delicate dance of flavors across the palate. During blind tastings these characteristics help quickly classify a wine as a warm or cool climate wine, and help identify exactly where a particular wine came from and how it grew up on the vine.

Climate

Beyond average temperature, climate takes into account the weather patterns and atmospheric conditions that can develop or destroy wine grapes. These factors include things like rainfall, humidity, wind, frost, hail, and quality of sunlight, which will impact everything from a grape's skin thickness (tannins!) to the effectiveness of anti-fungal chemical sprays designed to fight off vine mold.

Depending on what scientist you talk to (and how many glasses of wine they've had on that particular day), there are dozens of ways to classify climate: by average temperature (warm vs. cool climate), by scale (macroclimate, mesoclimate, microclimate), or by general climate groups (Mediterranean, Maritime, or Continental, for example). The best vintages usually result from stable climates that allow for slow, steady ripening, without heavy rainfall or extreme temperatures.

Elevation

From terraced sloping hills to deep down in the valley, elevation affects how grapes grow. High altitude does two things that benefit certain wines:

- cooler temperatures at night
- longer growing seasons

Chilly nights at high altitudes mean greater diurnal temperatures (the range between daytime and nighttime temperatures), which help grapes conserve their acidity and lead to more elegant, age-worthy wines. Moral of the story? Chilly nights on the vine, wine lives a long time.

Mountain and hillside vineyards also tend to receive more direct and concentrated sunlight (which leads to greater color concentration and stronger tannins).

Soil Type

As usual, dirt doesn't get the credit it deserves. Soil type – including sand, clay, dirt, pebbles, rocks, and dozens of combinations in between plays a big role in how grapes grow up and to the kinds of wine that they become. Soil type determines the availability of nutrients, water drainage, water retention, and can even moderate temperature in a vine's immediate microclimate.

Far from the nutrient-rich potting soil used for house plants, grape vines actually perform better when nutrients are scarce and roots aren't swampy. These conditions cause the vine to focus more energy on survival and less energy on growing grapes, which means that the vine gives off fewer clusters – and each grape has more character, concentration, and quality. As a result, sandy soil vineyards tend to produce more elegant wines than clay-based soils; and clay-based soils tend to produce bolder, more structured wines.

Geopolitics

In the world of wine, crossing borders is quite literally a game changer. While there exists universal consensus that wine is great, we don't all agree on how it should be made or what should be printed on the label. As far as wine is concerned, the laws of the land are usually designed to do one of two things:

- Fight against wine fraud (by standardizing wine labels, protecting designations of origin, and systems of wine classification), or
- Protect the consumer (by regulating additives and production procedures). It seems relatively straight forward, but the way it plays out in the real world is … somewhat maddening.

For example, in the US, in order for a wine to be labeled as a Pinot Noir varietal, it only needs to contain a minimum of 75% Pinot Noir. In Australia that benchmark is 85%, and in France, most bottles labeled "Bourgogne Rouge" are produced solely from Pinot Noir.

Not only does every country have its own rulebook (on the national, regional, and local level), but each country makes up their own regulatory systems for quality.

Variants of wine

Red wine

The red-wine production process involves extraction of color and flavor components from the grape skin. Red wine is made from dark-colored grape varieties. The actual color of the wine can range from violet, typical of young wines, through red for mature wines, to brown for older red wines. The juice from most purple grapes is actually greenish-white; the red color comes from anthocyan pigments (also called anthocyanins) present in the skin of the grape; exceptions are the relatively uncommon teinturier varieties, which actually have red flesh and produce red juice.

White wine

Fermentation of the non-colored grape pulp produces white wine. The grapes from which white wine is produced are typically green or yellow. Some varieties are well-known, such as the Chardonnay, Sauvignon, and Riesling. Other white wines are blended from multiple varieties; Tokay, Sherry, and Sauternes are examples of these. Dark-skinned grapes may be used to produce white wine if the wine-maker is careful not to let the skin stain the wort during the separation of the pulp-juice. Pinot noir, for example, is commonly used to produce champagne.

Dry (non-sweet) white wine is the most common, derived from the complete fermentation of the wort. Sweet wines are produced when the fermentation is interrupted before all the grape sugars are converted into alcohol. Sparkling wines, which are mostly white wines, are produced by not allowing carbon dioxide from the fermentation to escape during fermentation, which takes place in the bottle rather than in the barrel.

Rosé wine

A rosé wine incorporates some of the color from the grape skins, but not enough to qualify it as a red wine. It may be the oldest known type of wine, as it is the most straightforward to make with the skin contact method. The pink color can range from a pale orange to a vivid near-purple, depending on the varietals used and wine-making techniques. There are three primary ways to produce rosé wine: skin contact (allowing dark grape skins to stain the wort), saignée (removing juice from the must early in fermentation and continuing fermentation of the juice separately), and blending (uncommon and discouraged in most wine growing regions). Rosé wines can be made still, semi-sparkling, or sparkling, with a wide range of sweetness levels from dry Provençal rosé to sweet White Zinfandels and blushes. Rosé wines are made from a wide variety of grapes all over the world.

Fruit wines

Wines from other fruits, such as apples and berries, are usually named after the fruit from which they are produced combined with the word "wine" (for example, apple wine and elderberry wine) and are generically called fruit wine or country wine (not to be confused with the French term vin de pays). Other than the grape varieties traditionally used for wine-making, most fruits naturally lack either sufficient fermentable sugars, relatively low acidity, yeast nutrients needed to promote or maintain fermentation, or a combination of these three characteristics. This is probably one of the main reasons why wine derived from grapes has historically been more prevalent by far than other types, and why specific types of fruit wine have generally been confined to regions in which the fruits were native or introduced for other reasons.

Mead (honey wine)

Mead, also called honey wine, is created by fermenting honey with water, sometimes with various fruits, spices, grains, or hops. As long as the primary substance fermented is honey, the drink is considered mead. Mead was produced in ancient history throughout Europe, Africa and Asia, and was known in Europe before grape wine.

Starch-based "wine" and wine-based products

Other drinks called "wine", such as barley wine and rice wine (e.g. sake), are made from starch-based materials and resemble bee.

Main classification of wines

Depending upon the various attributes such as cultivar, stage of ripening of fruits, chemical composition of juice, use of additives to the must, vinification techniques and ageing of wine, the alcohol and sugar content, the wines are classified as natural wines (9-14 % alcohol) and dessert and appetizer wines (15-21 % alcohol). Dry wine, sweet table wine, specialty wine, champagne, muscat and burgundy wines are natural wines while sweet wine, cherries, vermouth and port wines are regarded as dessert and appetizer wines. The most famous types of wines are red and white wines, followed by rosé and sparkling wines.

There are other wine specialties around the world, such as the Portuguese Port Wine, a very rich flavor, often used by chefs in their signature dishes. Many types of wines can be divided into several groups, which are easy to remember. Depending upon product manufacturing all wines can be classified as grape wine, fruit wine, berry wine, vegetable wine, plant wine, raisin wine etc.

Grape wine is made exclusively from grapes and during the production process prohibited from using any other materials (exception is made only for sugar and oak barrels). Fruit wines are fermented alcoholic beverages made from a variety of base ingredients other than grapes; they may also have additional flavors taken from fruits, flowers, and herbs. These types of wines are made from pear, apple, banana, papaya, mango, jackfruit juice etc.

Cherry wine is produced from cherries, usually those cherries that provide sufficient acidity to wine. Plant wine is produced from juice of trees like maple, birch, melons, watermelons, and other garden plants such as rhubarb, parsnips and rose petals. Raisin wine is made from dried grapes (raisins). Multisort wine is produced by mixing different kinds of grapes and wine materials. Depending on the time of fermentation grape varieties and color fruit wines classified as are in red, white and pink wines.

Red wine

Red wine is made from red grapes, which are actually closer to black in color. There are many different types of red wines. This is considered to be the most classic in the kingdom of wines, mixing the delicious red grapes with a wide range of aromas, from oak to eucalypti, chocolate or even mint hints. The juice from most black grapes is greenish-white; the red colour comes from anthocyan pigments present in the skin of the grape.

Major types of red wine

There are six major categories of red wines. Barbera wine is prepared from red Italian grapes variety. It is popular table wine which is low in tannin and high in acidity with rounded fruitiness. This dry red wine pairs well with pizza, pasta with tomato-based sauce, hard cheeses. Merlot wine is very soft, having approachable flavors; descended from the Cabernet Franc grape and related to the Cabernet Sauvignon grape with a mild mix of plum and blackberry flavors.

Merlot pairs well with any dish. Shiraz wine (Syrah), is available with spicy flavors of blackcurrant and black pepper. It is served with meat dishes for better combination. Cabernet Sauvignon grape wine can be powerful and sharp, but silky and muted as it ages. It is one of the most famous types of wines in the world, especially among the French, Australians, Californians, and Chileans. Cabernet Sauvignon pairs perfectly with meat dishes like Sayrah. This sophisticated French wine is a mix of Cabernet Franc and Merlot, with a full-bodied taste of currant and bell pepper.

Malbec wine is a dry red wine known for its dark color and pronounced tannin. Another dry red wine is the Pinot Noir that is made from pinot noir black grapes. Noir is typically a light to medium bodied red wine that boasts considerable meal pairing versatility. This wine is rare and expensive. Zinfandel wine is produced from Zinfandel red grapes. This type of wine has high alcohol content, strong tannins and slightly spicy flavors.

White Wine

White wine is not exactly white; it is often yellow, gold or straw colored, depending on whether it includes the skin of the grape or just the juice. White wine can be made by the alcoholic fermentation of the non-colored pulp of green or gold colored grapes or from selected juice of red grapes, produced in Europe, and numerous other places such as Australia, California, New Zealand and South Africa and so on. It is treated so as to maintain a yellow transparent color in the final product. White wines often taste lighter, crisper and more refreshing than a red wine and so they often gain popularity during warmer months of the year. White wines are typically served alongside white meats and fish.

Major types of white wine

Chardonnay is a dry white from the Chardonnay grape, which is known for producing some of the finest white wines in the world, and is also used to make champagne. A dry white from the

Sauvignon Blanc grape is light yet acidic taste and as a great pair to salad and poultry dishes. Sauvignon Blanc grapes are often blended with Sémillon grapes to mellow the intensity.

Gewurztraminer is a mildly sweet white wine that has a smooth taste and deep aroma, ideal for sensitizing the palate before a meal. Muscat/Moscato wine is prepared from Muscat variety of grapes that smells like grapes, with a fruity, sweet flavor. A dry white made from the Pinot Gris grape, is one of the most delicious types of wine, rich in flavor and slightly spicy is called as Pinot Grigio wine. The taste of this wine varies from light and crisp to full and complex, based on where it is grown.

Reisling wine range from dry to sweet, but the Reisling grape tends to produce softer, fuller, fruitier wines, including ice wine, made from frozen grapes. Reisling wine comes with appetizing flavors of lime, apple and pear. A dry, sweet white wine that is often blended with a Sauvignon Blanc wine with very opposite flavor for a more rounded, balanced taste. It is called as Sémillon wine also used in fine dessert wines. Viognier wine, a dry white wine made from superior, rare grapes in the Rhône region of France. Viognier wine is best enjoyed before dinner.

Pink wine

Pink wine having a light pink color, grape skin removed immediately after the start of the fermentation process. These wines are made from a mixture of "black" and "white" grapes, using the technology of producing white wines.

Wines from tropical and subtropical fruits

Many tropical and subtropical fruits, including grapes, apples, pears, apricots, berries, peaches, cherries, oranges, mangoes, bananas and pineapples yield good amounts of juice on extraction. Upon fermentation, fruit juices can be changed into wines. However, the premium raw material for winemaking has been the grape, although attempts to process other fruit wines are being made.

The techniques used for the production of other fruit wines closely resemble those for the production of wines made from white and red grapes. The differences arise from two facts. It is somewhat more difficult to extract the sugar and other soluble materials from the pulp of some fruits than it is from grapes, and secondly the juices obtained from most of the fruits are lower in sugar content and higher in acids than is true for grapes. There are now solutions to this with the use of specialized equipment.

These types of wine includes, mango wine, banana wine, apple cider and wine.

Wine tasting

Wine tasting is the sensory examination and evaluation of wine. Many wineries provide tasting opportunities for customers and tourist alike and this has become a tradition. Wines contain many chemical compounds similar or identical to those in fruits, vegetables, and spices. The sweetness of wine is determined by the amount of residual sugar in the wine after fermentation, relative to the acidity present in the wine. Dry wine, for example, has only a small amount of residual sugar. Some wine labels suggest opening the bottle and letting the wine "breathe" for a couple of hours before serving, while others recommend drinking it immediately. Decanting (the act of pouring a wine into a special container just for breathing) is a controversial subject among wine enthusiasts. In addition to aeration, decanting with a filter allows the removal of bitter sediments that may have formed in the wine. Sediment is more common in older bottles, but aeration may benefit younger wines.

During aeration, a younger wine's exposure to air often "relaxes" the drink, making it smoother and better integrated in aroma, texture, and flavor. Older wines generally fade (lose their character and flavor intensity) with extended aeration. Despite these general rules, breathing does not necessarily benefit all wines. Wine may be tasted as soon as the bottle is opened to determine how long it should be aerated, if at all. When tasting wine, individual flavors may also be detected, due to the complex mix of organic molecules (e.g. esters and terpenes) that grape juice and wine can contain. Experienced tasters can distinguish between flavors characteristic of a specific grape and flavors that result from other factors in wine-making. Typical intentional flavor elements in wine—chocolate, vanilla, or coffee—are those imparted by aging in oak casks rather than the grape itself.

Vertical and horizontal tasting involves a range of vintages within the same grape and vineyard, or the latter in which there is one vintage from multiple vineyards. "Banana" flavors (isoamyl acetate) are the product of yeast metabolism, as are spoilage aromas such as "medicinal" or "Band-Aid" (4-ethylphenol), "spicy" or "smoky" (4-ethylguaiacol), and rotten egg (hydrogen sulfide). Some varieties can also exhibit a mineral flavor due to the presence of water-soluble salts as a result of limestone's presence in the vineyard's soil. Wine aroma comes from volatile compounds released into the air. Vaporization of these compounds can be accelerated by twirling the wine glass or serving at room temperature. Many drinkers prefer to chill red wines that are already highly aromatic, like Chinon and Beaujolais.

The ideal temperature for serving a particular wine is a matter of debate by wine enthusiasts and sommeliers, but some broad guidelines have emerged that will generally enhance the experience of tasting certain common wines. A white wine should foster a sense of coolness, achieved by serving at "cellar temperature" (13 °C (55 °F)). Light red wines drunk young should also be brought to the table at this temperature, where they will quickly rise a few degrees. Red wines are generally perceived best when served chambré ("at room temperature"). However, this does not mean the temperature of the dining room—often around 21 °C (70 °F)—but rather the coolest room in the house and, therefore, always slightly cooler than the dining room itself. Pinot noir should be brought to the table for serving at 16 °C (61 °F) and will reach its full bouquet at 18 °C (64 °F). Cabernet Sauvignon, zinfandel, and Rhone varieties should be served at 18 °C (64 °F) and allowed to warm on the table to 21 °C (70 °F) for best aroma.

Culinary uses of wines

Wine is a popular and important drink that accompanies and enhances a wide range of cuisines, from the simple and traditional stews to the most sophisticated and complex haute cuisines. Wine is often served with dinner. Sweet dessert wines may be served with the dessert course. In fine restaurants in Western countries, wine typically accompanies dinner. At a restaurant, patrons are helped to make good food-wine pairings by the restaurant's sommelier or wine waiter. Individuals dining at home may use wine guides to help make food–wine pairings. Wine is also drunk without the accompaniment of a meal in wine bars or with a selection of cheeses (at a wine and cheese party).

Wine is important in cuisine not just for its value as a drink, but as a flavor agent, primarily in stocks and braising, since its acidity lends balance to rich savory or sweet dishes. Wine sauce is an example of a culinary sauce that uses wine as a primary ingredient. Natural wines may exhibit a broad range of alcohol content, from below 9% to above 16% ABV, with most wines being in the 12.5–14.5% range. Fortified wines (usually with brandy) may contain 20% alcohol or more.

Religious significance

Ancient religions

The use of wine in ancient Near Eastern and Ancient Egyptian religious ceremonies was common. Libations often included wine, and the religious mysteries of Dionysus used wine as a sacramental entheogen to induce a mind-altering state.

Judaism

Wine is an integral part of Jewish laws and traditions. The Kiddush is a blessing recited over wine or grape juice to sanctify the Shabbat. On Pesach (Passover) during the Seder, it is a rabbinic obligation of adults to drink four cups of wine. In the Tabernacle and in the Temple in Jerusalem, the libation of wine was part of the sacrificial service. Note that this does not mean that wine is a symbol of blood, a common misconception that contributes to the Christian myth of the blood libel. "It has been one of history's cruel ironies that the blood libel—accusations against Jews using the blood of murdered gentile children for the making of wine and matzot— became the false pretext for numerous pogroms. And due to the danger, those who live in a place where blood libels occur are halachically exempted from using red wine, lest it be seized as "evidence" against them."

Christianity

In Christianity, wine is used in a sacred rite called the Eucharist, which originates in the Gospel account of the Last Supper (Gospel of Luke 22:19) describing Jesus sharing bread and wine with his disciples and commanding them to "do this in remembrance of me." Beliefs about the nature of the Eucharist vary among denominations.

While some Christians consider the use of wine from the grape as essential for the validity of the sacrament, many Protestants also allow (or require) pasteurized grape juice as a substitute. Wine was used in Eucharistic rites by all Protestant groups until an alternative arose in the late 19th century. Methodist dentist and prohibitionist Thomas Bramwell Welch applied new pasteurization techniques to stop the natural fermentation process of grape juice. Some Christians who were part of the growing temperance movement pressed for a switch from wine to grape juice, and the substitution spread quickly over much of the United States, as well as to other countries to a lesser degree. There remains an ongoing debate between some American Protestant Denomination.

Health Effects of Wine

Short-term effects

Wine contains ethyl alcohol, the same chemical that is present in beer and distilled spirits and as such, wine consumption has short-term psychological and physiological effects on the user. Different concentrations of alcohol in the human body have different effects on a person. The effects of alcohol depend on the amount an individual has drunk, the percentage of alcohol in the wine and the timespan that the consumption took place, the amount of food eaten and whether an individual has taken other prescription, over-the-counter or street drugs, among other factors. Drinking enough to cause a blood alcohol concentration (BAC) of 0.03%-0.12% typically causes an overall improvement in mood and possible euphoria, increased self-confidence and sociability, decreased anxiety, a flushed, red appearance in the face and impaired judgment and fine muscle coordination. A BAC of 0.09% to 0.25% causes lethargy, sedation, balance problems and blurred vision. A BAC from 0.18% to 0.30% causes profound confusion, impaired speech (e.g. slurred speech), staggering, dizziness and vomiting. A BAC from 0.25% to 0.40% causes stupor, unconsciousness, anterograde amnesia, vomiting, and death may occur due to inhalation of vomit (pulmonary aspiration) while unconscious and respiratory depression (potentially life-threatening). A BAC from 0.35% to 0.80% causes a coma (unconsciousness), life-threatening respiratory depression and possibly fatal alcohol poisoning. As with all alcoholic drinks, drinking while driving, operating an aircraft or heavy machinery increases the risk of an accident; many countries have penalties against drunk driving.

Wines can trigger the positive emotions in a short period of time, such as relaxed and comfortable. The context and quality of wine can affect the mood and emotions, too.

Long-term effects

Most significant of the possible long-term effects of ethanol, one of the constituents of wine. Consumption of alcohol by pregnant mothers may result in fetal alcohol spectrum disorders.

The main active ingredient of wine is alcohol, and therefore, the health effects of alcohol apply to wine. A 2016 systematic review and meta-analysis found that moderate ethanol consumption brought no mortality benefit compared with lifetime abstention from ethanol consumption. A systematic analysis of data from the Global Burden of Disease study found that consumption of ethanol increases the risk of cancer and increases the risk of all-cause mortality, and that the level of ethanol consumption that minimizes disease is zero consumption. Some studies have concluded that drinking small quantities of alcohol (less than one drink in women and two in men) is associated with a decreased risk of heart disease, stroke, diabetes mellitus, and early death. Drinking more than this amount actually increases the risk of heart disease, high blood pressure, atrial fibrillation, and stroke. Some of these studies lumped former ethanol drinkers and life-long abstainers into a single group of nondrinkers, hiding the health benefits of life-long abstention from ethanol. Risk is greater in younger people due to binge drinking which may result in violence or accidents. About 3.3 million deaths (5.9% of all deaths) are believed to be due to alcohol each year.

Alcoholism is a broad term for any drinking of alcohol that results in problems. It was previously divided into two types: alcohol abuse and alcohol dependence. In a medical context, alcoholism is said to exist when two or more of the following conditions is present: a person drinks large amounts over a long time period, has difficulty cutting down, acquiring and drinking alcohol takes up a great deal of time, alcohol is strongly desired, usage results in not fulfilling responsibilities, usage results in social problems.

Winery

A winery is a building or property that produces wine, or a business involved in the production of wine, such as a wine company. Some wine companies own many wineries. Besides wine making equipment, larger wineries may also feature warehouses, bottling lines, laboratories, and large expanses of tanks known as tank farms. Wineries may have existed as long as 8,000 years ago.

Ancient history

The earliest known evidence of winemaking at a relatively large scale, if not evidence of actual wineries, has been found in the Middle East. In 2011 a team of archaeologists discovered a 6000 year old wine press in a cave in the Areni region of Armenia, and identified the site as a small winery. Previously, in the northern Zagros Mountains in Iran, jars over 7000 years old were discovered to contain tartaric acid crystals (a chemical marker of wine), providing evidence of winemaking in that region. Archaeological excavations in the southern Georgian region of Kvemo Kartli uncovered evidence of wine-making equipment (containers called qvevri) dating back 8000 years. In 2017 the remnants of an 8000-year-old facility for large-scale production was found 20 miles south of Tbilisi, Georgia.

Purpose

Wineries typically employ winemakers to produce various wines from grapes by following the winemaking process. This process involves the fermentation of fruit, as well as blending and aging of the juice. The grapes may be from vineyards owned by the winery or may be brought in from other locations. Many wineries also give tours and have cellar doors or tasting rooms where customers can taste wines before they make a purchase. Winery architecture is very varied and rich and it is used by wineries as a way to promote their wines and cellar doors.

A class of winery license known as the farm winery allows farms to produce and sell wines on site. Farm wineries differ from commercial wineries in that the fruit which is the source of the wine is usually produced on the farm, and the final product is also sold on the farm.

Farm wineries usually operate at a smaller scale than commercial wineries. Farm wineries are a form of value added marketing, known as agritourism, for farmers who may otherwise struggle to show a profit.

A *micro-winery* is a small wine producer that does not have its own vineyard, and instead sources its grape product from outside suppliers. The concept is similar to a microbrewery, in that small batches of product are made primarily for local consumption. The concept of the micro-winery is not as easily accepted as that of the microbrewery, however, as the general public has been conditioned to associate a winery as having a vineyard. A winery uses similar wine-making equipment as a major commercial winery, just on a smaller scale. Glass carboys and sanitary plastic pails are often seen in the facilities of a micro-winery. Typically, each batch of wine yields 23 Liters (6 US gallons). One of the primary differences of a micro-winery as compared to a typical winery is that a micro-winery is typically able to offer a wider range of wines; as it is not tied to the grapes it grows.

The urban winery is a recent phenomenon whereby a wine producer chooses to locate their winemaking facility in an urban setting within a city rather than in the traditional rural setting near the vineyards. With advances in technology and transportation, it is not a problem for an urban winery to grow their grapes in a remote location and then transport them to the urban facility for crushing, fermentation and aging. Urban wineries have been opened in cities across the United States including San Francisco; Sacramento; Portland, Oregon; Seattle; Frederick, Maryland; New York; Cincinnati; San Diego; and Los Angeles to name a few.

Wine aficionados traditionally had to travel to remote areas to learn about winemaking firsthand and to taste the offerings of a wine producer in the setting in which they were made. Now, many urban dwellers can hop in their car for a short drive or take public transportation or even walk, and have an authentic winery experience. Many urban wineries offer productions tours and a traditional tasting room for this purpose and also offer retail sales. This allows the consumer to purchase directly from the source ensuring that wines have been stored correctly and not subjected to extreme conditions that can occur in transport which can occasionally result in spoiled wines.

A few urban wineries are also incorporating full-service restaurants or venues for live entertainment. Many also offer their customers the ability to make their own wine under the guidance of their winemaking team. Amateur winemakers can choose the grape varieties, select an appellation, make production decisions along the way and participate in the final blending, bottling and even design their own labels. This has spawned a new generation of boutique wines that are available in micro quantities as small as 30 bottles.

Winemaking and viniculture

The basic concept of wine, its history and its major composition has been discussed in the previous paragraphs but as a wine maker, it is very important to understand the basic process of wine making and all the stages involved in it before you can think of fine-tuning and discovering alternate ways by which you can boost your business.

Any one that makes wine is a wine maker or traditionally known as a vintner. Such persons are engaged in making wines and are generally employed by wineries or wine companies or can also have his own wine business. Wine making has been around for thousands of years just as wine itself. It is said to not only be an art but a science in itself as it involves a lot of bio chemical processes. Wine making is a natural process that requires little human intervention, but each wine maker guides the process through different techniques. Viticulture is the process of growing grapes, it involves a complex interaction (terroir) between the following factors:

Soil - Soil influences how much water and heat are available. Grapes need a steady, but not excessive, water supply.

- Color - Dark soils tend to be warmer than light soils because they are better at absorbing and holding heat.
- Geology - Rocky or stony soils allow water to drain better than clay soils; rocks also help to absorb heat in the soil.
- Chemicals - The role of chemicals in the soil is not clearly understood (see sidebar).
- Topography - This influences the amount of sunlight available (temperature) and the drainage (water supply).

Climate/Microclimate - This influences temperature, sunlight and water (rainfall, fog, mist). Some grapes, such as Vitis Vinifera, tend to grow best in areas where the seasonal temperature varies by about 30 to 35 degrees Fahrenheit (17 to 19 degrees Celsius).

The types of grapes that are planted and grown in any given area depend upon the terroir. In the Northern Hemisphere, grapes begin to bud in late March or early April. The grapes grow, bloom and develop fruit throughout the summer. The grower's goal is to keep the leaf growth small, which allows more sun in and keeps the grape clusters small yet numerous. The growers must also watch for signs of drought, disease and pests. In late September or early October, the grapes are ready to harvest. The actual times vary with the climate, latitude and judgment of individual growers.

In the fall, it is crush time. The grapes are harvested. Some vineyards use mechanical harvesting techniques, but most hire workers to pick the grapes by hand. The grapes are then brought to the winery. Many wineries are located on or near the vineyards. If the wineries are far away, the grapes are shipped in refrigerated trucks.

Once the grapes reach the winery, they get crushed. Inside the crusher, there is a perforated, rotating drum. The holes in the drum allow the juice and the skins of the grapes to pass through, but keep the stems inside the drum. The crushed grapes and juice are called *must*.

This leads us to the main wine making process which can also be called vinification and refers to the production of wine, starting with the selection of the fruit, its fermentation into alcohol, and the bottling of the finished liquid. The history of wine-making stretches over millennia. The science of wine and winemaking is known as oenology. Winemaking can be divided into two general categories: still wine production (without carbonation) and sparkling wine production (with carbonation — natural or injected). Red wine, white wine, and rosé are the other main categories. Although most wine is made from grapes, it may also be made from other plants, this is referred to as fruit wine. Other similar light alcoholic drinks (as opposed to beer or spirits) include mead, made by fermenting honey and water, and kumis, made of fermented mare's milk.

What happens next depends on the type of grape. Red-grape must is sent directly to the fermentation tanks. White-grape must is sent first to a wine press, where the juice is separated from the skins, because white wines are fermented from skinless grapes.

A wine press separates the juice from the skins. The wine press consists of a stainless steel cylinder with an inflatable rubber bladder inside. The must is poured inside the cylinder and the bladder is inflated with air. The bladder squeezes the skins against the side of the cylinder and forces the juices out. The juices are collected and sent to the fermentation tanks. At some wineries, the skins are recycled to local nurseries for fertilizer.

The must, whether from red grapes or pressed white grapes, is ultimately sent to the fermentation tanks. The fermentation tanks are airtight, made of stainless steel and can hold 1,500 or 3,000 gallons (5,678 or 11,356 liters). The tanks are cooled with glycol to maintain a temperature in the 40-F range (4-C range). The winemaker adds sugar and yeast to start the process of fermentation. The type of yeast and the amount of sugar added depends on the type of grape.

The process of fermentation

Fermentation is a viable technique in the development of new products with modified physicochemical and sensory qualities especially flavor and nutritional components. Alcohol, acetic and lactic acid fermentations are important for quality in production. Out of these, alcoholic fermentation is widely employed for the preparation of beverages in which alcohol is major constituent. Fermented beverages have been known to mankind from time immemorial. An alcoholic beverage is a drink that contains ethanol.

These are divided into three general classes for taxation and regulation of production namely beers, wines, and spirits distilled beverages such as whisky, rum, gin, vodka etc. Beer is made by fermentation of starch combining yeast and malted cereal starch, especially barley corn, rye, wheat or blend of several grains and usually flavored with hops. It contains 4 to 8 per cent alcohol and its energy value ranges between 28 and 73 kcal per 100 mL. Distilled alcoholic beverages are produced by distilling ethanol by fermentation of grains, fruits or vegetables. They are made from sugarcane juice, molasses, fermented mash of cereals and potatoes and fermented malt of barley and rye.

The alcohol content in distilled alcoholic beverage ranges between 40 and 60 per cent. Fruit wines are un-distilled alcoholic beverages usually made from grapes or other fruits such as peaches, plums or apricots, banana, elderberry or black current etc. which are nutritive, more tasty and mild stimulants. These fruits undergo a period of fermentation and ageing. They usually have an alcohol content ranging between 5 to 13 percent. Wines made from fruits are often named after the fruits. No other drinks, except water and milk have earned such universal acceptance and esteem throughout the ages as has wine. Wine is a food with a flavor like fresh fruit which could be stored and transported under the existing conditions.

Being fruit based fermented and un-distilled product, wine contains most of the nutrients present in the original fruit juice. The nutritive value of wine is increased due to release of amino acids and other nutrients from yeast during fermentation. Fruit wines contain 8 to 11 per cent alcohol and 2 to 3 per cent sugar with energy value ranging between 70 and 90 kcal per 100 mL.

Basically, fermentation requires two things: sugars and yeasts. A ripe organic grape is full of natural sugars and there are wild yeasts living on its skin. As soon as the skin of the grape is broken, fermentation can begin. To make wine, all the winemaker has to do is collect his grapes and gently crush them, releasing the sugary juice and exposing it to the yeasts.

Fermentation will continue until all the sugar has been turned into alcohol or the level of alcohol in the juice reaches around fifteen percent, whichever is sooner. At around fifteen percent alcohol, the yeasts will die naturally and any leftover sugars will remain in the wine.

Yeasts

A natural wine is fermented only with the wild yeasts native to its terroir. Yeast strains vary widely from place to place and contribute significantly to the odour of the finished wine. The yeasts indigenous to a particular area are an important part of what gives its wines their character. Conventionally grown grapes have little or no wild yeast living on their skin. The winemaker will kill whatever yeast remains with sulphur dioxide, and reseed the grapes with a single strain of commercially produced yeast.

Wines fermented in this way have less personality, all using the same few commercial yeast strains, and are less an expression of their terroir. This is one reason they taste so similar. They are also less complex, as each of the many wild yeasts present on an organic grape will contribute something to the finished wine.

Sugars

The level of alcohol in the finished wine is determined by the level of sugar in the grapes from which it is made. More sugar means there is more for the yeast to convert into alcohol. Grapes grown further north see less sun and therefore contain less stored sugar than those grown in the south. Traditionally, therefore, northern wines contain a lower level of alcohol.

Chaptalization is a way of boosting the level of alcohol in the finished wine by adding sugar to the juice during fermentation. The technique is named after Jean Antoine Chaptal, Napoleon's minister for agriculture, who is said to have invented it.

Note though, that a natural wine is fermented only with its own sugars.

Malolactic fermentation

This occurs when lactic acid bacteria metabolize malic acid and produce lactic acid and carbon dioxide. This is carried out either as an intentional procedure in which specially cultivated strains of such bacteria are introduced into the maturing wine, or it can happen by chance if uncultivated lactic acid bacteria are present.

Malolactic fermentation can improve the taste of wine that has high levels of malic acid, because malic acid, in higher concentration, generally causes an unpleasant harsh and bitter taste sensation, whereas lactic acid is gentler and less sour. Lactic acid is an acid found in dairy products. Malolactic fermentation usually results in a reduction in the amount of total acidity of the wine. This is because malic acid has two acid radicals (-COOH) while lactic acid has only one. However, the pH should be monitored and not allowed to rise above a pH of 3.55 for whites or a pH of 3.80 for reds. pH can be reduced roughly at a rate of 0.1 units per 1 gram/litre of tartaric acid addition.

The use of lactic acid bacteria is the reason why some chardonnays can taste "buttery" due to the production of diacetyl by the bacteria. Most red wines go through complete malolactic fermentation, both to lessen the acid of the wine and to remove the possibility that malolactic fermentation will occur in the bottle. White wines vary in the use of malolactic fermentation during their making. Lighter aromatic wines such as Riesling, generally do not go through malolactic fermentation. The fuller white wines such as barrel fermented chardonnay, are more commonly put through malolactic fermentation. Sometimes a partial fermentation, for example, somewhere less than 50% might be employed.

Once the fermentation process is completed, red wines are sent to the press to separate the skins from the wine. The red wines are then filtered to remove the yeast. White wines are allowed to settle and are filtered to remove the yeast. Once the yeasts are removed, the wines are stored in either stainless steel storage tanks or oak barrels (oak gives many wines a characteristic flavor) depending on the type of wine. In some red wines, a second type of fermentation, called malolactic fermentation, is undertaken while in storage as explained above. The aging process begins here.

SULFITES

Sulfur-containing compounds called sulfites are naturally found on grapes to retard the growth of bacteria and mildew. Most winemakers add sulfites to the wine to help stabilize it as it ages. However, some people are allergic to sulfites -- wines that are labelled as sulfite-free have had the sulfites chemically removed.

After the wine has aged sufficiently, as determined by the winemaker, it is time to bottle and package it for sale. The operator pumps the wine from the storage tank to the bottling machine. There, bottles are loaded by hand and a pre-measured amount of wine flows into each bottle. After each bottle is filled, the operator removes it and places it in the corking machine. The machine draws a vacuum inside the bottle that sucks the pre-loaded cork into the neck of the bottle.

After the bottle is corked, the operator places the neck into the foil machine, which seals an aluminum foil wrapper over the cork. Next, the operator moves the bottle to the labelling machine, where the winery's self-adhesive label is placed on the bottle. Finally, the operator loads the bottle into a case for shipping and distribution.

Natural winemaking is a style loosely defined as using native yeasts in the fermentation process and minimal or no sulfur dioxide in the winemaking process. It may also mean unfined and unfiltered as well.

Natural winemaking is not governed by laws in the U.S. and has no inspection or verification process unless it is a biodynamic wine.

Natural winemakers may use organic or biodynamic grapes in their wines. Using native yeasts and relying on minimal manipulation often means that wines have a varying profile from year to year. Different vintages vary more than conventionally made wine because of the non-interventionist approach. This is a key part of the natural wine aesthetic which emphasizes the least amount of intervention

In conclusion, wine making occurs in five different stages;

Harvesting

Harvesting is the first step in the wine making process and an important part of ensuring delicious wine. Grapes are the only fruit that have the necessary acids, esters, and tannins to consistently make natural and stable wine. Tannins are textural elements that make the wine dry and add bitterness and astringency to the wine.

The moment the grapes are picked determines the acidity, sweetness, and flavor of the wine. Determining when to harvest requires a touch of science along with old fashioned tasting. The acidity and sweetness of the grapes should be in perfect balance, but harvesting also heavily depends on the weather.

Harvesting can be done by hand or mechanically. Many wine makers prefer to harvest by hand because mechanical harvesting can be tough on the grapes and the vineyard. Once the grapes are taken to the winery, they are sorted into bunches, and rotten or under ripe grapes are removed.

Crushing and Pressing

After the grapes are sorted, they are ready to be de-stemmed and crushed. For many years, men and women did this manually by stomping the grapes with their feet. Nowadays, most wine makers perform this mechanically. Mechanical presses stomp or trod the grapes into what is called must. Must is simply freshly pressed grape juice that contains the skins, seeds, and solids. Mechanical pressing has brought tremendous sanitary gain as well as increased the longevity and quality of the wine.

For white wine, the wine maker will quickly crush and press the grapes in order to separate the juice from the skins, seeds, and solids. This is to prevent unwanted color and tannins from leaching into the wine. Red wine, on the other hand, is left in contact with the skins to acquire flavor, color, and additional tannins.

Fermentation

After crushing and pressing, fermentation comes into play. Must (or juice) can begin fermenting naturally within 6-12 hours when aided with wild yeasts in the air. However, many wine makers intervene and add a commercial cultured yeast to ensure consistency and predict the end result.

Fermentation continues until all of the sugar is converted into alcohol and dry wine is produced. To create a sweet wine, wine makers will sometimes stop the process before all of the sugar is converted. Fermentation can take anywhere from 10 days to one month or more.

Clarification

Once fermentation is complete, clarification begins. Clarification is the process in which solids such as dead yeast cells, tannins, and proteins are removed. Wine is transferred or "racked" into a different vessel such as an oak barrel or a stainless steel tank. Wine can then be clarified through fining or filtration.

Fining occurs when substances are added to the wine to clarify it. For example, a wine maker might add a substance such as clay that the unwanted particles will adhere to. This will force them to the bottom of the tank. Filtration occurs by using a filter to capture the larger particles in the wine. The clarified wine is then racked into another vessel and prepared for bottling or future aging.

Aging and Bottling

Aging and bottling is the final stage of the wine making process. A wine maker has two options: bottle the wine right away or give the wine additional aging. Further aging can be done in the bottles, stainless steel tanks, or oak barrels. Aging the wine in oak barrels will produce a smoother, rounder, and more vanilla flavored wine. It also increases wine's exposure to oxygen while it ages, which decreases tannin and helps the wine reach its optimal fruitiness. Steel tanks are commonly used for zesty white wines.

After aging, wines are bottled with either a cork or a screw cap, depending on the wine maker's preference.

Organically produced wine

According to beveragedaily.com, for a growing number of wine producers, organic is not just an expanding market to tap into: it is a fundamental philosophy of their business and a necessity for the longevity of their enterprise and land.

Organic wine is wine made from grapes grown in accordance with principles of organic farming, which typically excludes the use of artificial chemical fertilizers, pesticides, fungicides and herbicides. EU laws state that organic wine is made from grapes grown organically. Organic farming presumes that no harmful pesticides, herbicides, fungicides and chemical fertilizers are allowed to grow the grapes.

Research has shown that grapes are amongst other fruit that store those harmful substances, hence it is increasingly beneficial for your health to drink wines made from organic grapes. It also generally means no artificial or synthetic preservatives were used, no colors added and no agents added to alter the taste. If you are wondering, organic also means nothing genetically modified.

There's loads of restrictions when it comes to organic wine. So what's permitted?

Organic wine permits naturally occurring substances: elemental sulphur and salt copper sulphate (Bordeaux mixture). Plant oils, seaweed, powders based on wild herbs do not enter vine's sap or grape pulp and thus have no effect on the resulting wine. Organic farming focuses on the techniques that are focused on prevention rather than cure. Don't you think it is a way forward?

The main nutrient added to the soil is compost as it is an organic fertilizer. It allows slow release of soil minerals and nutrients by encouraging an array of living organisms, so in a nutshell it feeds the soil, not the plants.

It also means that vine roots penetrate deeper into the soil and thus said to make the wines taste more complex. Critics sometimes add that noticeable mineralogy of the wine is a sign of how well this wine expresses the soil and terroir.

EU laws state that organic wine is made from grapes grown organically. Organic farming presumes that no harmful pesticides, herbicides, fungicides and chemical fertilizers are allowed to grow the grapes. Research has shown that grapes are amongst other fruit that store those harmful substances, hence it is increasingly beneficial for your health to drink wines made from organic grapes. It also generally means no artificial or synthetic preservatives were used, no colors added and no agents added to alter the taste. If you are wondering, organic also means nothing genetically modified.

The consumption of organic wine grew at a rate of 3.7 percent over the year ending September 19, 2009 out-pacing growth in the consumption of non-organic wine which grew 2% during a similar period. There are an estimated 1500–2000 organic wine producers globally, including negociant labels, with more than 885 of these organic domains in France alone. These figures indicates that it is rapidly getting recognized worldwide.

Wine production comprises two main phases - that which takes place in the vineyard (i.e. grape growing) and that which takes place in the winery (i.e. fermentation of the grapes into wine, bottling etc.). The baseline definition of organic wine as "wine made with grapes farmed organically", deals only with the first phase (grape growing). There are numerous potential inputs which can be made during the second phase of production in order to ferment and preserve the wine. The most universal wine preservative is sulphur dioxide. The issue of wine preservation is central to the discussion of how organic wine is defined.

Wine matures over time, and it is widely considered that certain types of wines improve with aging, as the flavors become more integrated and balanced. As a result, the greatest percentage of wines are produced in a way that allows them to last, sometimes as long as decades. The use of added sulfites is debated heavily within the organic winemaking community. Many vintners favor their use for stabilization of wine, while others frown on them. Currently the only effective preservatives that allow wines to last for a long period are 'non-organic'. While there are a growing number of producers making wine without added preservatives, it is generally acknowledged that these wines are for consumption within a few years of bottling.

The various legal definitions of organic wine serve to address this challenge regarding the use of preservatives. In wine produced in the European Union, addition of sulphites, used as presevatives, are allowed in organic wine, but at lower maximum levels than in conventional wine production. In other countries the preservative is not allowed at all in organic wine. In the

United States, wines certified "organic" under the National Organic Program cannot contain added sulfites, but wines labelled as "wine made from organic grapes" can. Depending on your country of residence, it is important to follow these legal definitions/ restrictions in the making of wine commercially, so as to avoid running into trouble with authorities in charge.

In 2017, according to the survey "Le bio, c'est bon pour l'emploi" conducted by the UMR Moisa (Supagro Montpellier/Inra), an organic wine farm creates 1.5 times more jobs than a non-organic wine farm. Another finding is that jobs in this sector are more stable. 34.6% of organic farms employ one or more permanent employees against 21.6% in the case of non-certified farms. Similarly, 71.49% of employees are full-time, compared to 66.83% on non-organic farms.

Can organic wines be said to be biodynamic or natural?

The answer is actually a big No. these two terms are quite different themselves. Although they are also better alternatives to regular produced wines, they may not be organic. Actually, biodynamic wines are closer to being referred to more organic than natural wines. Let's understand them better!

Biodynamic wines

Biodynamic wines are wines made employing biodynamic methods both to grow the fruit and during the post-harvest processing. Biodynamic wine production uses organic farming methods (e.g. employing compost as fertilizer and avoiding most pesticides) while also employing soil supplements prepared according to Rudolf Steiner's formulas, following a planting calendar that depends upon astronomical configurations, and treating the earth as "a living and receptive organism".

Biodynamic methods are used in viticulture in a variety of countries, including France, Switzerland, Italy, Spain, Austria, Germany, Australia, Chile, South Africa, Canada, and the United States. In 2013 over 700 vineyards worldwide comprising more than 10,000 ha/24,710 acres were certified biodynamic.

A number of very high-end, high-profile commercial growers have converted recently to biodynamic practices. According to an article in Fortune, many of the top estates in France, "including Domaine Leroy in Burgundy, Château de la Roche-aux-Moines in the Loire, Maison Chapoutier in the Rhone Valley, and Domaine Zind-Humbrecht in Alsace," follow biodynamic viticulture. For a wine to be labeled "biodynamic" it has to meet standards laid down by the Demeter Association, an internationally recognized certifying body.

Biodynamic agriculture is based on the work of Rudolf Steiner (1861–1925), who gave Agriculture Course in 1924, predating most of the organic movement. It includes ecological principles, emphasizing spiritual and mystical perspectives. Biodynamics aims at the ecological self-sufficiency of farms as cohesive, interconnected living systems.

Some grape growers who have adopted biodynamic methods claim to have achieved improvements in the health of their vineyards, specifically in the areas of biodiversity, soil fertility, crop nutrition, and pest, weed, and disease management. For example, the late Anne-Claude Leflaive of Domaine Leflaive estate in Burgundy claimed that the use of biodynamic methods saved a badly diseased vineyard, to the point that it now produces some of her most highly prized wines.

A long-term study of one California winery found that improved quality for both biodynamic and organic could not be explained. This study in different vineyard blocks at a commercial vineyard in Ukiah, California found no difference between biodynamic methods with general organic farming methods with respect to soil quality, nor in the yield per vine, clusters per vine, and cluster and berry weight. However, one of the authors, Leo McCloskey has made the case that consumer quality scores, 100-point scores, are expected to be higher for both biodynamic and organic over traditional farming.

Biodynamic winemakers claim to have noted stronger, clearer, more vibrant tastes, as well as wines that remain drinkable longer. Biodynamic wines are more "floral", according to Spanish biodynamic vintner Pérez Palacios.Biodynamic producers also claim that their methods tend to result in better balance in growth, where the sugar production in the grapes coincides with physiological ripeness, resulting in a wine with the correct balance of flavor and alcohol content, even with changing climate conditions.

In a blind tasting of 10 pairs of biodynamic and conventionally made wines, conducted by Fortune and judged by seven wine experts including a Master of Wine and head sommeliers, nine of the biodynamic wines were judged superior to their conventional counterpart. The biodynamic wines "were found to have better expressions of terroir, the way in which a wine can represent its specific place of origin in its aroma, flavor, and texture." Critics caution that such comparisons of wines of the same type need to be controlled for differences in soil and subsoil, and the farming and processing techniques used.

Critics acknowledge the high quality of biodynamic wines, but question whether many of the improvements in vineyard health and wine taste would have happened anyway if organic farming were used, without the mysticism and increased effort involved in biodynamics. Other critics attribute the success of biodynamic viticulture to the winemakers' higher craftsmanship and meticulous attention to detail. Ray Isle, managing editor of Wine & Spirit magazine, says, "So what if they also think burying cow horns full of manure will help them channel new life forces from the cosmos?"

Natural wines

Natural wines are the ones that are made without major intervention during the winemaking process. Natural wines are not necessarily made from organic grapes, and at the same time organic wines are mostly about the grapes and not what happens in the winery. The latter process is exactly how you should differ these two kinds of wines - organic is about the grape, natural is about what happens at the winery.

One major difference here is the addition of sulphites - natural wines have no added sulphites, just naturally occurring ones. Organic wines will have less sulphites than conventional wines, but winemakers can still use them in minimal quantities (up to 100mg/l).

Benefits of organically produced wine

Common sense tells us that if organic wine contains less toxins (nasty man-made like pesticide residues and more), then it is better for you.

To go beyond your own health, you are also contributing to a cleaner, healthier and more sustainable environment.

We all know that red wine contains resveratrol, which is an antioxidant that protects against cancer, heart disease, is anti-ageing and may even extend your lifespan. You can imagine that pesticides can significantly decrease the potency of any antioxidant. In fact, the French government in 2012 officially released a statement that there is a link between pesticides and Parkinson's disease in agricultural workers.

In addition to that research from the Department of Human Nutrition at the University of Southampton, University of Rome's Clinical Nutrition, University of California at Davis and University of Newcastle showed that organic wines are richer in nutrients and antioxidants. Natural and sulphite free wines have generally lighter effect and better consumed by your liver.

There is an ongoing debate on wine, its benefits and harm, whether organic wines are better or not. Regardless of that, many people make a conscious decision to buy organic products not just to better nourish themselves, but also because they are being environmentally responsible.

LEAN MANUFACTURING

Lean manufacturing or lean production is a systematic method originating in the Japanese manufacturing industry for the minimization of waste (無駄 muda) within a manufacturing system without sacrificing productivity, which can cause problems. Lean also takes into account waste created through overburden (無理 muri) and unevenness in workloads (斑 mura). Working from the perspective of the client who consumes a product or service, "value" is any action or process that a customer would be willing to pay for.

Lean Manufacturing is, therefore, all about the optimizing processes and eliminating waste. These seemingly simple efforts can greatly help with cutting costs while still delivering high-quality product customers want and are willing to pay for.

The Lean approach is based on thoroughly evaluating your process to find what you're doing right and remove or adapt all steps that may be possibly generating waste. This waste is called muda and encompasses anything that doesn't add value to the end product.

It's essential to stress that cutting costs according to what Lean proposes doesn't mean compromising the quality of the product in any way. You'll only cut costs by finding better, more efficient ways to do the same things.

By adopting a lean philosophy, you enjoy the benefit of continuous improvement. It means that instead of making rapid, irregular and abrupt changes that are disruptive to the workplace, you'll make small and sustainable changes. By doing so you'll ensure that the people who actually work with these processes, equipments, and materials will take the changes forward.

A brief history of lean from Toyota

Toyota's development of ideas that later became lean may have started at the turn of the 20th century with Sakichi Toyoda, in a textile factory with looms that stopped themselves when a thread broke. This became the seed of autonomation and Jidoka. Toyota's journey with just-in-time (JIT) may have started back in 1934 when it moved from textiles to produce its first car. Kiichiro Toyoda, founder of Toyota Motor Corporation, directed the engine casting work and discovered many problems in their manufacturing. He decided he must stop the repairing of poor quality by intense study of each stage of the process. In 1936, when Toyota won its first truck contract with the Japanese government, his processes hit new problems and he developed the "Kaizen" improvement teams.

Levels of demand in the Post War economy of Japan were low and the focus of mass production on lowest cost per item via economies of scale therefore had little application. Having visited and seen supermarkets in the USA, Taiichi Ohno recognized the scheduling of work should not be driven by sales or production targets but by actual sales. Given the financial situation during this period, over-production had to be avoided and thus the notion of Pull (build to order rather than target driven Push) came to underpin production scheduling.

It was with Taiichi Ohno at Toyota that these themes came together. He built on the already existing internal schools of thought and spread their breadth and use into what has now become the Toyota Production System (TPS). It is principally from the TPS (which was widely referred to in the 1980s as just-in-time manufacturing), but now including many other sources, that lean production is developing.

The concept of Lean manufacturing

James Womack's first mentioned the concept of Lean manufacturing in his 1990' book, "The Machine That Changed the World".

It was defined as a theory that could help simplify and organize your work environment to reduce waste and keep your people, equipment and workspace responsive to what's needed right now. So, how can you reduce waste and do things more efficiently without compromising the quality of the result? On top of it all, how can you keep up with the changing demands to respond as fast as possible?

Waste costs you and, consequently, your customer's money. If your waste is responsible for making your customers pay more for your product/service, they might go elsewhere that delivers the same quality at a lower price. Being competitive in a market where everyone else is also fighting to stay competitive requires a lot of flexibility (aka being able to respond as fast as possible to changes in demand).

Focus on the customer

To find the efficiencies, lean manufacturing adopts a customer-value focus. It consists in asking "What is your customer willing to pay for? What does the customer value?"

Customers want value, and they'll only pay if the value your product/service offers can meet their needs. They shouldn't pay for defects, or for the extra cost of having large inventories, for example.

In other words, they shouldn't pay for your production problems or for the unnecessary waste you generate. As I pointed out before, waste is anything that doesn't add value to the end product. There are eight categories* of waste that you should monitor:

Categories of waste:

Overproduction: Are you producing the right amount to meet your consumers demand or are you going overboard and generating unnecessary storage costs?

Waiting: How much lag time is there between your production steps? Does someone have to wait for someone else to finish a task before they can begin theirs? Idle time means you're paying for an employee to stay there doing nothing while he/she waits.

Inventory (work in progress): Are your supply levels and work in progress inventories too high? Do you buy too much raw material that needs to be stored for a while before it's used?

Transportation: Do you move materials efficiently? Are you working with the transportation alternatives that offer the best rates?

Over-processing: Do you work on the product too many times, or otherwise work inefficiently?

Motion: Do people and equipment move between tasks efficiently?

Defects: How much time do you spend finding and fixing production mistakes?

Workforce: Do you use workers efficiently?

The first seven sources of waste were originally outlined in the Toyota production system (TPS) and were called muda. Lean Manufacturing often adds the eighth "workforce" category.

Lean prioritizes simple, small, and continuous improvements. Instead of revolutions, focus on changing one small thing at a time, such as changing the placement of a button on a page. Do it one step at a time.

As these small improvements are added together, they can lead to a higher level of efficiency throughout the whole system.

There are some essential tools that make up the lean manufacturing system. These tools work hand in hand in achieving the overall objectives of any producer.

25 ESSENTIAL LEAN TOOLS

5S

What is 5S?

Organize the work area:

Sort (eliminate that which is not needed)

Set In Order (organize remaining items)

Shine (clean and inspect work area)

Standardize (write standards for above)

Sustain (regularly apply the standards)

How does 5S help?

Eliminates waste that results from a poorly organized work area (e.g. wasting time looking for a tool).

ANDON

What is Andon?

Visual feedback system for the plant floor that indicates production status, alerts when assistance is needed, and empowers operators to stop the production process.

How does Andon help?

Acts as a real-time communication tool for the plant floor that brings immediate attention to problems as they occur – so they can be instantly addressed.

BOTTLENECK ANALYSIS

What is Bottleneck Analysis?

Identify which part of the manufacturing process limits the overall throughput and improve the performance of that part of the process.

How does Bottleneck Analysis help?

Improves throughput by strengthening the weakest link in the manufacturing process.

CONTINOUS FLOW

What is Continuous Flow?

Manufacturing where work-in-process smoothly flows through production with minimal (or no) buffers between steps of the manufacturing process.

How does Continuous Flow help?

Eliminates many forms of waste (e.g. inventory, waiting time, and transport).

GEMBA (The Real Place)

What is Gemba?

A philosophy that reminds us to get out of our offices and spend time on the plant floor – the place where real action occurs.

How does Gemba help?

Promotes a deep and thorough understanding of real-world manufacturing issues – by first-hand observation and by talking with plant floor employees.

HEIJUNKA (Level Scheduling)

What is Heijunka?

A form of production scheduling that purposely manufactures in much smaller batches by sequencing (mixing) product variants within the same process.

How does Heijunka help?

Reduces lead times (since each product or variant is manufactured more frequently) and inventory (since batches are smaller).

HOSHIN KANRI (Policy Deployment)

What is Hoshin Kanri?

Align the goals of the company (Strategy), with the plans of middle management (Tactics) and the work performed on the plant floor (Action).

How does Hoshin Kanri help?

Ensures that progress towards strategic goals is consistent and thorough – eliminating the waste that comes from poor communication and inconsistent direction.

JIDOKA (Autonomation)

What is Jidoka?

Design equipment to partially automate the manufacturing process (partial automation is typically much less expensive than full automation) and to automatically stop when defects are detected.

How does Jidoka help?

After Jidoka, workers can frequently monitor multiple stations (reducing labor costs) and many quality issues can be detected immediately (improving quality).

JUST-IN-TIME (JIT)

What is Just-In-Time?

Pull parts through production based on customer demand instead of pushing parts through production based on projected demand. Relies on many lean tools, such as Continuous Flow, Heijunka, Kanban, Standardized Work and Takt Time.

How does Just-In-Time help?

Highly effective in reducing inventory levels. Improves cash flow and reduces space requirements.

KAIZEN (Continuous Improvement)

What is Kaizen?

A strategy where employees work together proactively to achieve regular, incremental improvements in the manufacturing process.

How does Kaizen help?

Combines the collective talents of a company to create an engine for continually eliminating waste from manufacturing processes.

KANBAN (Pull System)

What is Kanban?

A method of regulating the flow of goods both within the factory and with outside suppliers and customers. Based on automatic replenishment through signal cards that indicate when more goods are needed.

How does Kanban help?

Eliminates waste from inventory and overproduction. Can eliminate the need for physical inventories (instead relying on signal cards to indicate when more goods need to be ordered).

KPIs (Key Performance Indicators)

What are KPIs?

Metrics designed to track and encourage progress towards critical goals of the organization. Strongly promoted KPIs can be extremely powerful drivers of behavior – so it is important to carefully select KPIs that will drive desired behavior.

How do KPIs help?

The best manufacturing KPIs:

Are aligned with top-level strategic goals (thus helping to achieve those goals)

Are effective at exposing and quantifying waste (OEE is a good example)

Are readily influenced by plant floor employees (so they can drive results)

MUDA (Waste)

What is Muda?

Anything in the manufacturing process that does not add value from the customer's perspective.

How does Muda help?

It doesn't. Muda means 'waste'. The elimination of muda (waste) is the primary focus of lean manufacturing.

Overall Equipment Effectiveness (OEE)

What is Overall Equipment Effectiveness?

Framework for measuring productivity loss for a given manufacturing process. Three categories of loss are tracked:

Availability (e.g. downtime)

Performance (e.g. slow cycles)

Quality (e.g. rejects)

How does Overall Equipment Effectiveness help?

Provides a benchmark/baseline and a means to track progress in eliminating waste from a manufacturing process. 100% OEE means perfect production (manufacturing only good parts, as fast as possible, with no downtime).

PDCA (Plan, Do, Check, Act)

What is PDCA?

An iterative methodology for implementing improvements:

Plan (establish plan and expected results)

Do (implement plan)

Check (verify expected results achieved)

Act (review and assess; do it again)

How does PDCA help?

Applies a scientific approach to making improvements:

Plan (develop a hypothesis)

Do (run experiment)

Check (evaluate results)

Act (refine your experiment; try again)

POKA-YOKE (Error Proofing)

What is Poka-Yoke?

Design error detection and prevention into production processes with the goal of achieving zero defects.

How does Poka-Yoke help?

It is difficult (and expensive) to find all defects through inspection, and correcting defects typically gets significantly more expensive at each stage of production.

ROOT CAUSE ANALYSIS

What is Root Cause Analysis?

A problem solving methodology that focuses on resolving the underlying problem instead of applying quick fixes that only treat immediate symptoms of the problem. A common approach is to ask why five times – each time moving a step closer to discovering the true underlying problem.

How does Root Cause Analysis help?

Helps to ensure that a problem is truly eliminated by applying corrective action to the "root cause" of the problem.

Single-Minute Exchange of Dies (SMED)

What is Single-Minute Exchange of Dies?

Reduce setup (changeover) time to less than 10 minutes.

Techniques include:

Convert setup steps to be external (performed while the process is running)

Simplify internal setup (e.g. replace bolts with knobs and levers)

Eliminate non-essential operations

Create Standardized Work instructions

How does Single-Minute Exchange of Dies help?

Enables manufacturing in smaller lots, reduces inventory, and improves customer responsiveness.

SIX BIG LOSSES

What is Six Big Losses?

Six categories of productivity loss that are almost universally experienced in manufacturing:

Breakdowns

Setup/Adjustments

Small Stops

Reduced Speed

Startup Rejects

Production Rejects

How does Six Big Losses help?

Provides a framework for attacking the most common causes of waste in manufacturing.

SMART Goals

What are SMART Goals?

Goals that are: Specific, Measurable, Attainable, Relevant, and Time-Specific.

How do SMART Goals help?

Helps to ensure that goals are effective.

STANDARDIZED WORK

What is Standardized Work?

Documented procedures for manufacturing that capture best practices (including the time to complete each task). Must be "living" documentation that is easy to change.

How does Standardized Work help?

Eliminates waste by consistently applying best practices. Forms a baseline for future improvement activities.

TAKT TIME

What is Takt Time?

The pace of production (e.g. manufacturing one piece every 34 seconds) that aligns production with customer demand. Calculated as Planned Production Time / Customer Demand.

How does Takt Time help?

Provides a simple, consistent and intuitive method of pacing production. Is easily extended to provide an efficiency goal for the plant floor (Actual Pieces / Target Pieces).

Total Productive Maintenance (TPM)

What is Total Productive Maintenance?

A holistic approach to maintenance that focuses on proactive and preventative maintenance to maximize the operational time of equipment. TPM blurs the distinction between maintenance and production by placing a strong emphasis on empowering operators to help maintain their equipment.

How does Total Productive Maintenance help?

Creates a shared responsibility for equipment that encourages greater involvement by plant floor workers. In the right environment this can be very effective in improving productivity (increasing up time, reducing cycle times, and eliminating defects).

VALUE STREAM MAPPING

What is Value Stream Mapping?

A tool used to visually map the flow of production. Shows the current and future state of processes in a way that highlights opportunities for improvement.

How does Value Stream Mapping help?

Exposes waste in the current processes and provides a roadmap for improvement through the future state.

VISUAL MAPPING

What is Visual Factory?

Visual indicators, displays and controls used throughout manufacturing plants to improve communication of information.

How does Visual Factory help?

Makes the state and condition of manufacturing processes easily accessible and very clear – to everyone.

As with every approach towards improving production there are usually criticisms that follows. You as wine maker will then weigh your pros and cons and decide if lean manufacturing is worth trying and finding ways to pay attention to the problems highlighted and work on the criticisms it has in such a way that it does not play huge roles in your production methods.

Criticism

One criticism of lean is that its practitioners may focus on tools and methodologies rather than on the philosophy and culture of lean. Consequently, adequate management is needed in order to avoid failed implementation of lean methodologies. Another pitfall is that management decides what solution to use without understanding the true problem and without consulting shop floor personnel. As a result, lean implementations often look good to the manager but fail to improve the situation.

In addition, many of the popular lean initiatives, coming from the TPS, are solutions to specific problems that Toyota was facing. Toyota, having an undesired current condition, determined what the end state would look like. Through much study, the gap was closed, which resulted in many of the tools in place today. Often, when a tool is implemented outside of TPS, a company believes that the solution lay specifically within one of the popular lean initiatives. The tools which were the solution to a specific problem for a specific company may not be able to be applied in exactly the same manner as designed. Thus, the solution does not fit the problem and a temporary solution is created vs. the actual root cause.

The lean philosophy aims to reduce costs while optimizing and improving performance. Value stream mapping (VSM) and 5S are the most common approaches companies take on their first steps towards making their organization leaner. Lean actions can be focused on the specific logistics processes, or cover the entire supply chain. For example, you might start from analysis of SKUs (stock keeping units), using several days to identify and draw each SKUs path, evaluating all the participants from material suppliers to the consumer. Conducting a gap analysis determines the company's 'must take' steps to improve the value stream and achieve the objective. Based on that evaluation, the improvement group conducts the failure mode effects analysis (FMEA), in order to identify and prevent risk factors. It is crucial for front-line workers to be involved in VSM activities since they understood the process and can directly increase the efficiency. Although the impact may be small and limited for each lean activity, implementing a series small improvements incrementally along the supply chain can bring forth enhanced productivity.

After adopting the lean approach, both managers and employees experience change. Therefore, decisive leaders are needed when starting on a lean journey. There are several requirements to control the lean journey. First and most importantly, experts recommend that the organization have its own lean plan, developed by the lean Leadership. In other words, the lean team provides suggestions for the leader who then makes the actual decisions about what to implement. Second, coaching is recommended when the organization starts off on its lean journey. They will impart their knowledge and skills to shopfloor staff and the lean implementation will be much more efficient. Third, the metrics or measurements used for measuring lean and improvements are extremely important. It will enable collection of the data required for informed decision-making by a leader. One cannot successfully implement lean without sufficient aptitude at measuring the process and outputs. To control and improve results going forward, one must see and measure, i.e. map, what is happening now.

Lean manufacturing is different from lean enterprise. Recent research reports the existence of several lean manufacturing processes but of few lean enterprises. One distinguishing feature opposes lean accounting and standard cost accounting. For standard cost accounting, SKUs are difficult to grasp. SKUs include too much hypothesis and variance, i.e., SKUs hold too much indeterminacy. Manufacturing may want to consider moving away from traditional accounting and adopting lean accounting.

THINKING "LEAN" IN WINE MAKING

Lean production arose as a step towards a new era in production systems. It is a working philosophy designed to produce better products using fewer resources to obtain greater benefits. It has been applied to a wide variety of sectors different from the original automotive industry, in which it was developed. However, its application to continuous manufacturing processes of continuous products has been less, especially to the wine production sector.

The wine sector differs greatly to the automobile sector in various fundamental aspects but it also has common fundamental aspects in its production and logistics systems. An important part of this work has consisted in studying the wineries of the Rioja region. Research shows that most of the production problems in the wine sector can be tackled using a lean production system, making certain adjustments according to the type of production.

All wineries share a common objective – to create more output (at the same or better quality) with less inputs. The adoption of Lean Production techniques and practices can help wineries reduce costs and improve productivity by delivering tangible outcomes including: » Elimination of waste & non-value-adding activities » Streamlining of processes (Flow) » Shifting of business model from supply-focused to demand-focused » Improved resource efficiency, elimination of waste and cost savings through reduced purchase of raw materials » Faster production lead times » Elimination of losses and deterioration of material while processing » Reductions in the amount of information between processes » Improvements in the use of limited physical space and machinery in the winery » Improved distribution of work among operators.

Recent case studies have demonstrated that applying Lean Production practices to wineries can achieve, on average: » Reduction in materials costs of between 8-16%, » Reduction in production lead-time between 50-65%. Asides from the productivity-related benefits, Lean Production can assist wineries with improving their environmental sustainability performance.

The successful implementation of Lean Production can be achieved through adhering to five key principles:

1. For each product family, define value from the standpoint of the end customer.

2. Identify all the value-adding steps in the value stream for each product family, and eliminate the non-value-adding steps.

3. Organize the value-creating steps to occur in a smooth flow.

4. Allow customers to 'pull' value from upstream activity.

5. As value is defined, value-adding steps are identified, non-value-adding steps are removed, and flow and pull are introduced, repeat the process and foster continuous improvement towards the ultimate goal of creating perfect value with no waste.

Start thinking lean

The simplest way for wineries to begin adopting Lean Production is to start 'thinking lean' – that is, getting in the right frame of mind to begin identifying opportunities to reduce waste and improve productivity. To that end, there are two important techniques that enable wineries to begin to 'think lean'. The first technique relates to the selection of key metrics that define efficiency and productivity in wine production. Many businesses that have embarked on the journey of adopting Lean have jumped straight into the application of its tools and concepts without knowing what drives performance in each aspect of winery operations, or how this performance is measured. Without this knowledge, wineries won't know where best to apply the Lean tools or whether their application has made a positive impact on the business. The second technique, Seven Waste Identification, is core to Lean Production and helps to identify, characterize and address seven types of waste that are used to describe non-value-adding activities in any winery operation:

1. Waste of Overproduction

2. Waste of Waiting

3. Waste of Transportation (Conveyance)

4. Waste of Over-processing

5. Waste of Inventory

6. Waste of Motion

7. Waste of Correction (Defects)

SELECTING AND USING THE RIGHT METRICS FOR MEASURING LEAN & PRODUCTIVITY

The first step in adopting a lean mindset is understanding 'which metrics matter' in tracking and improving productivity in winery operations, and ensuring that these metrics are considered front-of-mind when adopting Lean Production techniques and practices. Wineries can choose from a variety of metrics to use as indicators of how effective Lean techniques and practices are at improving overall business performance Production metrics commonly used by the wine industry, and worthy of consideration when implementing Lean Production practices include: » Net operating profit ($) » Operational Costs (OPEX$) per litre of wine » Operational Costs (OPEX$) per $ of Revenue » Litre (L) wine per work order » Tonnes of grape crush per week (i.e. during vintage).

Lean Production tools such as the 25 that has been mentioned above use a variety of metrics to measure the performance of a production system, however two that are of particular importance are:

1. Takt time

2. Overall Equipment Effectiveness (OEE)

Takt time is how often one part or product should be produced, based on the rate of sales, to meet customer requirements. Takt time can be used as a reference to match the pace of work to the average pace of customer demand. Takt time is often used in Value Stream Mapping, Standard Work, Total Productive Maintenance and Pull Systems. The basic calculation for Takt time is as follows,

$$\text{Takt time} = \frac{Available\ working\ time\ per\ day}{Customer\ demand\ rate\ per\ day}$$

Takt time can be used to calculate bottling and packaging rates. It can also be used for internal processes. For example, Takt time can be applied to receival, destemming, crushing, and pressing steps. Using the Takt formula the 'quantity of must pressed per day' becomes the 'customer demand rate.

Overall Equipment Effectiveness (OEE) can be used to indicate the overall effectiveness of a piece of production equipment, or an entire production line. OEE consists of three components: » Performance %, which grades the actual output of the piece of equipment or production line, with what it should be producing (<100% means that there are speed losses). » Availability %, which grades how much time is available to run the machine versus actual machine run-time (<100% means that there are losses associated with downtime e.g. from machine breakdowns or set-up time). » Quality %, which compares the performance of the piece of equipment or product line in creating an output to quality specifications (for example <100% means that the machine or production line didn't make juice or wine to specification). Together these components, when multiplied together, form the OEE, OEE (%) = Performance% x Availability% x Quality%.

IDENTIFYING THE SEVEN WASTE

In order to identify wasteful activity, we need to understand what's useful versus non-useful in the wine production process, which can be described as being made up of three key of types of activities:

» Value Added (VA) – activities performed in the process that the customer is willing to pay-for (i.e. that directly relate to the product quality and characteristics)

» Business Value Added (BVA) – activities necessary to maintain the business

» Non-Value Added (NVA) – activities that do not add value to the output product, and don't have a valid business reason for being performed. Lean Production techniques and practices focused on eliminating NVA activities and optimizing BVA activities, such that the maximum amount of time, attention and resources can be focused on the VA activities.

The seven waste has been stated earlier on and would now be explained elaborately

1. WASTE OF OVERPRODUCTION

There are two types of Overproduction waste:

1) Producing more output than is necessary

2) Producing output at a rate faster than is required.

Overproduction is arguably the most important type of waste for a winery to tackle as it usually compounds the occurrence of other types of wastes, such as a requirement to store more wine for longer periods of time (Waste of Inventory), or increased risk of quality issues (Waste of Correction). It's also one of the more difficult types of waste to deal with in the industry, as both the seasonal nature of wine and the commercial arrangements that many wineries have with vineyards (locked-in to long-term contracts to purchase a minimum amount of grapes) mean that wineries are obliged to make batch volumes of wine, irrespective of projected demand in wine from year to year. Causes of Overproduction in wineries include: » Inaccurate forecasting based on varying customer demand » Contracts with vineyards requiring the purchase of grapes at tonnage levels that are far in excess of projected demand » Dealing with low-quality fruit, for which wineries convert into a saleable wine, however due to the lack of quality more time is required to sell the wine (and usually at lower margins) » Making more wine than is needed 'in order to keep busy' » Optimizing one part of production (i.e. making it faster) without having a broader view of what the entire production process needs » Bottling wine to reduce ullage.

2. WASTE OF WAITING

The waste of Waiting happens every time staff or operators experience idle time because certain information, equipment, processes, tools or instructions from senior management (e.g. from the winemaker) isn't ready for them to access. This waste is sometimes difficult to see, given that staff in particular usually find something else to do to 'keep busy'. This isn't necessarily a good thing -- keeping busy on the wrong tasks can sometimes cause more trouble than simply doing nothing. The waste of Waiting can affect the business through increased operating costs, strained capacity and higher overtime costs in situations where wine production needs to work harder to make-up for lost time and make weekly or monthly targets. This can ultimately affect the winery's ability to control quality, manage staff and reduce the winery's responsiveness to deal with changing customer demands. Causes of Waiting in wineries include: » Delays from suppliers (e.g. grape supply from vineyards) » Mismanagement of production scheduling » Equipment break-downs at key bottlenecks of wine production (e.g. pressing) » Equipment at capacity » Delays in arrival of tanker (for off-site bottling) » Busy winemakers (e.g. resulting in delays with inspecting wine quality and advising on production schedule) » Waiting for information to arrive » Waiting for customers to arrive (e.g. cellar door).

EXAMPLES OF WAITING IN WINERIES: » Production staff waiting for winemakers to be available to answer production- and quality-related questions » Production staff waiting for equipment to be fixed so as to re-commence with production » Sales staff waiting for wine to be bottled, particularly if bottled off site » Tanker waiting for wine to be ready for loading (i.e. for off-site bottling) » Production staff and winemaker waiting for lab test results (quality testing) » Accounts department waiting for winery to have their books up to date by the end of each month » Waiting for cellar door customers to arrive

3. WASTE OF TRANSPORTATION (CONVEYANCE)

The waste of Transportation is defined as the movement of wine and materials within production that adds no value to the product. This movement may be achieved via the use carts or forklifts, through conveyor belts, extended pipework or manually by staff. This type of waste can have a significant impact on a winery's productivity, such as creating delays in production (due to transportation time), creating potential safety hazards, and costing the business through labour and equipment costs required to move the material around. Causes of Transportation in wineries: » Inefficient/outdated winery plant/production layout » Reliance on forklifts or carts to move materials around site » Warehousing with large inventories » Off-site storage (requirement for additional transport).

EXAMPLES OF TRANSPORTATION IN WINERIES: » Transferring of finished wine to storage tanks (which may be located some distance from the point of production) » Transferring of finished wine onto tanker, and transported to off-site bottling facility » Transportation of grape marc to offsite facility » Warehousing (movement of finished wine to and from warehousing facility) » Transportation and movement of product for sales events such as trade shows (including return of un-sold product).

4. WASTE OF OVER-PROCESSING

The waste of Over-processing occurs when aspects of the wine production process are designed or operated in such a way that it uses more space, resources and/or time than what is actually required. This type of waste may result from equipment working faster than necessary, processes that use more production staff/operators than what is truly required, or even quality assurance or administrative processes that use more paperwork and man-hours than what is needed. The cost of Over-processing waste can be measured in terms of operational costs consumed over the course of production (such as energy, space, labor or equipment utilisation). The less processing required to deliver wine to the customer, the more productive the winery.

Causes of Over-processing in wineries: » Lack of formal process scheduling » Lack of standards associated with production specifications, quality assurance » No implementation of production and equipment control/automation » Overly complex administrative procedures » Lack of internal and external communication (expectations of what is required vs not required).

EXAMPLES OF OVER-PROCESSING IN WINERIES: » Wine production finishing steps such as filtration are repeated or excessively conducted due to lack of formal or standardized monitoring/quality checks » Critical equipment (e.g. refrigeration systems) running harder than they need to in order to meet the minimum acceptable product specifications » Use of manual administration systems leading to complex and duplicated paper work, rather than making use of centralized customer relationship management systems (e.g. EasyWine, TallEmu) to provide a whole-of-business management package.

5. WASTE OF INVENTORY

The waste of Inventory relates to the excess amount of product (wine-in-tank, or wine-inbottle) or material on-hand other than what's needed to satisfy current customer demand. Excess inventory has a significant impact on a winery's cash-flow position (essentially it's money tied-up in product that has not yet been sold). The better a winery can manage its inventory, the healthier the business will look on the balance sheet. For wineries, Inventory can be sub-divided into three types: » Cycle stock – inventory needed to cover normal demand. The amount of cycle stock to hold can be calculated by multiplying the average daily demand for product by the lead-time to replenish the stock. » Buffer stock – this inventory is kept to account for any unexpected surges in customer demand. The amount of buffer stock to keep depends on a variety of factors, but can be estimated based on probabilities or historical records. » Safety stock – this inventory is kept to protect supply to the customer from product spoilage/breakage, loss or other external factors.

Causes of Inventory in wineries: The main cause relates to overproduction of wine associated with excess grapes arriving during vintage, leading to significant stores of wine-in-tank, however there may also be other causes a winery should consider, such as: » Unlevelled/choppy production schedules » Transportation constraints » Optimistic demand forecasts.

EXAMPLES OF INVENTORY IN WINERIES: » Overproduction leading to significant levels of inventory – have to buy a certain amount of fruit regardless of quality » Excessive levels of wine labels (old, out-of-date wine labels that are no longer useful) » Additional materials (e.g. additions, or spare parts) ordered well-beyond the amount needed in the near future.

6. WASTE OF MOTION

The waste of Motion relates to all the manual activity that production or administration staff undertake to complete a task – whether it be managing equipment, searching for tools or materials, or accessing important information. Whatever it may be, any movement by staff that doesn't add value to the wine production process is a waste of time, and hence a waste of money to the business. Studies have shown that in a disorganized production-based workplace, up to 10% of the working day can be spent searching for items or changing-over equipment/product batches – eliminating this waste can result in significant improvements to staff productivity.

Causes of Motion in wineries: » Poorly designed processes » Lack of standard work methods

EXAMPLES OF MOTION IN WINERIES: » Searching for misplaced tools or testing equipment during production » Double-handling of materials and paper work » Production staff walking the office to obtain production information (rather than having the information accessible in the production area and updated daily).

7. WASTE OF CORRECTION (DEFECTS)

The waste of Correction relates to the additional work and effort required to correct wine product that does not meet a sufficient standard of quality to suit customer and winemaker expectations. Causes of Correction in wineries: » Lack of process checks at all stages of wine production » Low-quality materials from suppliers (e.g. grapes, dry goods) » Inadequate training and work instructions.

EXAMPLES OF CORRECTION IN WINERIES: » Poor fruit quality leading to increased effort to convert into a saleable wine » Having to re-do jobs in the winery, such as filtration and stabilization (if standard filtration practices and monitoring haven't been adhered to, and stabilization has not worked properly) » Relabeling wines » Stock accuracy – having to write-off stock every time an inventory check is conducted creates a significant amount of re-work for administration staff – typically the result of staff not accurately logging stock.

Identifying waste in the production process

Waste identification is fundamental to Lean Production. Many of the key Lean Production tools and techniques focus on the identification and elimination of waste of one type or another, however there are two simple techniques that are ideal for wineries to begin using immediately, irrespective of their level of prior knowledge:

1. 5S, which is a 5-step approach to achieve and maintain a high level of workplace organization.

2. Value Stream Mapping (VSM), which is a visual tool that helps to identify and communicate causes of waste and opportunities for improvement.

These techniques are easy and straightforward to use, and can be introduced immediately to a winery operation with little prior knowledge. Applying these tools alone will lead to significant opportunities in reducing waste and improving productivity.

5S WORKPLACE PRODUCTIVITY

5S is a Lean Production methodology that can be used by wineries to expose wasteful practices and inefficiencies, and achieve and maintain a high level of workplace organisation. It consists of 5 key steps that can be applied to any working area of a winery – from wine production and tank farms/storage through to warehousing and grape receival, administration and cellar door.

KEY STEPS OF 5S

1. Sort and eliminate items that are not needed

2. Straighten and organize all items that remain

3. Sweep and ensure the workplace is organized

4. Standardize to ensure that waste and inefficiencies are easily and consistently recognized

5. Sustain the previous four steps and make 5S a way of life in the business.

Important to note is that 5S offers much more than good housekeeping and keeping things tidy – it provides the means to foster a workplace culture of efficiency, waste identification and to some extent, workplace pride. Successfully applied, 5S can deliver significant benefits to a winery, such as improved staff productivity, improved workflow and process efficiency, and a safer workplace environment.

VALUE STREAM MAPPING

A value stream can be defined as all the steps taken – both value-adding and non-value-adding – to convert grapes into a bottle or case of wine. Value Stream Mapping (VSM) is a visual tool that can assist wineries with plotting all the activities required to receive and fulfill a request from our customer.

It provides the visual means to: » Identify causes of waste such as Overproduction, Waiting, Unnecessary Processing, Motion etc. » Identify opportunities to reduce waste, improve flow and better balance production across equipment and labor, and » Communicate the process, performance and characteristics of a winery's operations such that anyone across the business can understand and discuss using a common language. The Value Stream Mapping (VSM) process consists of two types of maps:

1. Current-state VSM – describes the current performance and characteristics of the winery operation's value stream.

2. Future-state VSM – describes the future performance of the winery operation's value stream if improvements were made to the winery's production processes to smoothen flow, reduce waste and shift from a push-based production system to a pull-based production system.

IMPLEMENT WASTE ELIMINATION PRACTICES

STANDARD WORK

STANDARD WORK CAN BE USED TO REDUCE THESE TYPES OF WASTE: Waste of overproduction, Waste of inventory, Waste of waiting, Waste of motion, Waste of transportation (conveyance), Waste of correction (defects), and Waste of over processing. Standard Work basically means developing and complying with a 'standard' at which the work should be undertaken. Another way of thinking about this is that 'work' will be undertaken to a certain 'standard'. Wineries stand to benefit from standard work through: » Reduced costs » Waste elimination » Stabilized workflow » Increased productivity » Simplifying processes for existing and new staff Creating 'standard work' is not difficult to implement, just so long as two key objectives are met:

a) A standard is developed for the work

b) Staff and processes comply with the standard.

Creating standard work requires three components:

1. A work rate (Takt time)

2. A work sequence

3. Adequate resources for a smooth workflow (i.e. avoiding stops and starts).

Before a standard is implemented, it needs to be identified, confirmed as reasonable and fair by all involved in the process, needs to be understood and needs commitment by the organization to maintain this standard. Once this standard work has been implemented, it is important to continuously monitor its effectiveness and incrementally improve on this standard.

STANDARD WORK PREREQUISITES

There are some pre-requisites for creating standard work:

1. A stable process: Standard work requires a stable process. By stable process we are referring to stable material, equipment and workforce. In the wine industry, seasonal and grape variety variations do have an impact on the volume of work, but not the stability of the process. Wine manufacture follows a standard pattern despite these minor variations.

2. Leadership prerequisites: Standardized work requires that four leadership prerequisites be met before standard work can be implemented. » The organization needs to adopt a blame free culture. This doesn't mean being accountability-free, but it does mean suspending all judgment and focusing on problems with the process, before looking at the person. Creating an environment where staff feel empowered to make decisions and are confident to contribute to the working environment is key for implementing standard work. » The organization requires a commitment to continuous improvement. This needs to be led from the highest level of leadership. » Leaders need to be out on the floor to understand how the business is performing.

The use of visual management controls can help leaders understand business performance. » Leaders and staff need to quickly respond to issues and not be delayed in raising these issues. Undertaking these leadership styles ensures standard work has the most chance of succeeding and reducing wastes within a winery.

TYPES OF STANDARDISED WORK

There are 3 main classes of standard work Type 1 – Repetitive single cycle processes Type 2 – Short but variable cycles Type 3 – Long cycle standard work.

The repetitive single cycle process work of a Type 1 standard work may involve an operator or robot packing at a bottling line. The short but variable cycles of Type 2 work may include large components of vintage production (crushing, pumping, filtering, etc). Type 3 the long cycle standard work may include the yearly cycle of work that needs to be undertaken from vintage to vintage. Understanding the type of standardized work helps select the appropriate metrics work rate (Takt time), work sequence, and adequate resources for a smooth workflow.

TOOLS FOR STANDARDISED WORK

There are five main tools for developing standardized work. These are:

1. Time Observation record

2. Equipment process capacity table

3. Standardized work/walk combination sheet

4. Standardized work map

5. Standardized Work Instruction Sheet

These tools rely on each other and the end goal is producing a standardized Work Instruction Sheet. This sheet forms part of a visual management tool that can help both operators and leaders maximize process efficiencies and eliminate waste.

TOTAL PRODUCTIVE MAINTENANCE (TPM)

TPM can be used to reduce these types of waste: » Waste of waiting » Waste of inventory » Waste of transportation (conveyance) » Waste of motion Total productive maintenance (TPM) is a set of techniques to ensure that machines in a production process are always able to perform their required tasks. This technique involves getting all staff involved in maximizing equipment running time. TPM is more than just keeping a good maintenance schedule, but another way of looking at increasing process efficiencies and minimizing waste and downtime. The simple rule for TPM is that it refuses to accept that machines will inevitably fail. The main goal of TPM is to enhance the volume of the production, employee morale and job satisfaction.

BENEFITS OF TPM

There are five main benefits that wineries can gain from TPM: » A reduction in the total life-cycle costs of equipment » Operators become equipment maintainers » Maintainers become improvers » It is a reminder that equipment should not fail » It reduces downtime and waste.

ERROR PROOFING

Error proofing can be used to reduce these types of waste: » Waste of overproduction » Waste of inventory » Waste of waiting » Waste of motion » Waste of transportation (conveyance) » Waste of correction (defects) » Waste of over processing Error-proofing refers to the implementation of fail-safe mechanisms to prevent a process from producing defects or other problems.

The idea behind error proofing is even very small numbers of defects are not acceptable. The only way to achieve this goal is to prevent mistakes from happening in the first place. Error-proofing becomes a method of inspection at the source instead of down the line at final product quality control.

By the time an error is detected in the final product, many resources have already been wasted in creating a final, but unacceptable product. Achieving high levels of process capability requires this type of focus on prevention rather than detection.

Everyday examples: There are lots of examples from everyday life for error-proofing devices » Plugging a cord into a power point » Most computer cables » Automatic stop when you open a microwave door » Childproof caps on medicine bottles » Different nozzles on petrol and diesel pumps » Not being able to start an automatic car out of 'park' They are everywhere! They stop people from making careless mistakes and more importantly, protect people, processes, equipment, quality, and reduce waste.

Examples in wineries: » Optical checking for wine levels in a bottle » Bar code readers to track batches » 'Lock outs' that prevent equipment being activated if conditions are not correct » Hose connections to ensure only the correct medium is transported (e.g. gas, water, wine, etc)

When choosing to error proof, is it important to identify if this will be necessary. Not all processes can or need to be error-proofed. A three-step analysis of the risks can help both identify the need for a) error proofing and b) the form of the error proofing. These three steps are:

1. Identification of the need

2. Identification of possible mistakes

3. Management of mistakes before satisfying the need. Undertaking these three steps allows methods to be used to identify the need and the control for a situation. Error proofing needs to be related to the magnitude of the risk. For example, connecting a pump the wrong-way-round is unlikely to cause any issues – the wine wont pump, but time will be lost by needing to reconnect the pump the correct way.

Connecting a red wine pump to a white wine tank however can cost hundreds of thousands of dollars in both lost material and disposal costs. Both of these systems need controls, but the consequence for one outweighs the other.

FAST CHANGEOVERS

Fast changeovers can be used to reduce these types of waste: » Waste of waiting » Waste of inventory » Waste of transportation (conveyance) » Waste of motion. A fast changeover is the process of converting a line, machine or tank from running one product to another. Changeover times can last from a few minutes to as much as several weeks depending on the process. The purpose for reducing changeover time is not to increase production capacity, but to allow for more frequent changeovers. This increases production flexibility.

BENEFITS OF FAST CHANGEOVERS

The benefits for fast changeovers include: 1. A reduction of lead time. This means goods can be created (i.e. wine transferred from tank to a finished bottle) in a short amount of time when an order is placed by the customer. This is in contrast to having a large inventory of boxed finished wine in anticipation of a customer order. 2. Reduced lot sizes. If the changeover is fast, a winery can switch from one product to another with little time loss. If the changeover is long, a business is more likely to change products only once every few days. This can be a challenge when customers want different varieties and not high volumes of one stock. 3. Fast changeovers increase flexibility. A dynamic winery can deal with changes more rapidly than a static winery. This can lead to significant increases in performance. 4. Fast changeover greatly reduces inventory. Products are only created on demand and so inventory is low. This significantly reduces inventory costs and increases cash flow. 5. Quick changeover increases production flow leveling. Processes are more constant and less interrupted.

STEPS TO ENSURE FAST CHANGEOVERS

1. Machines cannot be idle

2. The best setup time is no setup time

3. Tools needed for changeover are ready to be used

4. Sufficient staff are available to minimize changeover time

5. A shared goal for all team members is reducing setup time

6. If possible and safe, start changeover while equipment is still active (i.e. prepare tools, parts etc ready for changeover while line is running). This is also known as an external setup.

The following are general guidelines that can improve changeover time: » Identify internal setups – these are steps that are undertaken when a machine has stopped (e.g. physically changing a hose connection). Where possible, try and convert these to external setups or reduce the time that equipment will be idle (e.g. get the next hose connection ready for changeover so the only internal step is changing a coupling). » Eliminate non-essential operations – this may include only changing one side of a guard rail instead or replacing the guard rail altogether. » Perform the external setup ready for changeover – this may include getting tools, guides, and staff ready for changeover and ensuring all equipment is present and ready. » Simplify the internal setup - this may mean changing screw connectors to clamps or quick grips systems. » Measure – The only way to understand if a change in process has decreased or increased the setup time is to measure the new process.

VISUAL MANAGEMENT

Visual management can be used to reduce these types of waste: » Waste of overproduction » Waste of inventory » Waste of waiting » Waste of motion » Waste of transportation (conveyance) » Waste of correction (defects) » Waste of over processing Visual management is a broad concept that relies on that fact that people generally understand conditions better when they are represented visually. Simple information representation is more likely to be understood by staff than complicated information. For example, put someone in a room with 1 button and 1 red light. Give them the instructions to push the button when the red light turns on. This is fairly simple and requires very little instruction. Now, put someone in the cockpit of the space shuttle Atlantis. Ask them to fire thrusters to correct orbit for re-entry trajectory. A few questions come to mind. Which button is that? How do I know what my current orbit is?

When do I stop? How do I wake up from this nightmare? For a trained astronaut, this process may be relatively simple, but this takes years of training.

Visual management removes the clutter and helps people make clear decisions on the steps needed for the situation on hand.

KEY BENEFITS OF VISUAL MANAGEMENT

The key benefits to visual management include: » Highlighting critical information in ways that cannot be ignored. » Help expose, prevent and eliminate waste. » Prevent information overload so employees can see their results. » Significantly reduce the time needed to understand information. » Increase a company's profitability. Many of the standard tools are visual management guides. These are presented for the purpose of visually guiding an operator's work flow and time to perform tasks. It is also a visual tool to allow leaders to ensure work is being performed to standard and to look for ways to improve the process. As mentioned above, visual management may be as simple as a red light which lets an operator know when to act. It is important not to overexpose staff to visual management tools, otherwise we can get lost in the information again. Too much information is just as bad as too little. Examples of visual management may also include tools like shadow boards which indicate where a tool is located and if a tool is missing. The main objective of visual management is to clarify information to allow then to work efficiently.

QUALITY CONTROL TOOLS

Quality control can be used to reduce these types of waste: » Waste of overproduction » Waste of inventory » Waste of waiting » Waste of motion » Waste of transportation (conveyance) » Waste of correction (defects) » Waste of over processing In this context, quality is about delivering products that customers will purchase at an optimum cost effectiveness.

Quality is more than just inspecting goods at the end of a production line, but is the sum of tasks throughout a process which leads to quality. In the pursuit of quality, an organisation needs commit to continuous improvement. Quality throughout an organisation decreases costs as no rework needs to be undertaken. When quality is applied through all aspects of an organisation, it may also be referred to as Total Quality Management (TQM). Data can be captured throughout the wine making process to deliver important information as to how the winery is performing.

To a large extent, the chemical changes within a winery are usually captured through the laboratory or via remote testing. Other areas of a winery may require additional data to be recorded such as the number of barrels washed per day, the number of breakdowns per month, etc. An important step in quality is capturing this data so it can be measured, managed, and visually communicated for all to see.

RE-THINKING PRODUCTION FLOW

The ultimate objective of Lean Production is to provide maximum value to the customer with zero waste. In all, a variety of relatively simple concepts, techniques, practices and tools were covered that assist with identifying and eliminating waste within the existing "batch-and-push" production model that is inherent in the winemaking process. This step will introduce a more challenging set of techniques that, if used appropriately, can shift the production model towards one that is pull-based, where the winery is only producing wine at the pace that the customer demands it. Specifically, the techniques covered in this Step include: » Producing to Takt Time » Supermarkets and production signalling » Controlling the 'pacemaker' process » Leveling production » Future-state Value Stream Mapping. It must be noted that there are some inherent characteristics of wine production that can make the introduction of pull-based production systems very challenging, and in some cases impossible. Some of these characteristics include: » The fact that vintage only happens for a few months of the year, meaning that supply of grapes occurs in batches (creating Waste of Overproduction) » Many wine variants require a period of maturation before final filtration and bottling/ packaging, which disrupts the continuous flow of wine production from grape to bottle and leads to big inventories » Transport of finished wine can only happen in batches, due to the distance from the winery (regional) to distributors and end-customers (typically metropolitan).

Hence for some wineries, the techniques described in this step may not be considered suitable. Having said this, wineries can still benefit from investigating and hypothesizing how they may apply – the investigation process alone usually yields opportunities for improvement. In particular, wineries with significant bottling and packaging facilities will tend to get the most out of these techniques.

KEEPING IT UP: CONTINUOUS IMPROVEMENT

Continuous improvement (CI) (or 'Kaizen', in Lean terminology) is an incremental way of improving processes and practices over time throughout the winery, and in particular making continued use of the Lean Production techniques and tools covered in all the steps so that improvements are made permanent to the business. Hence CI is relevant to all Lean Production tools and techniques as an overlapping concept and set of guidelines for wineries to adopt in order to gain the maximum benefit from Lean.

STEPS FOR CONTINUOUS IMPROVEMENT

At the core of the continuous improvement process is the approach that lots of small improvements increases the overall efficiency of the business. There are three broad steps to this approach:

1. Examine the process

2. Identify improvement opportunities

3. Implement the changes. Using these three broad steps, there are two main barriers and these include a) time needed to examine the process and b) time needed to implement the changes. How often do we hear someone say, "There must be a better way to do this." These people are correct – there is always a better way to do it, but staff need to feel both empowered and capable to a) identify the issues and b) implement the change.

In addition to the three broad steps, there are six additional mindsets that are needed for continuous improvement: 1. Small changes 2. Ideas from workers 3. Spend small 4. Use your existing skill set 5. Self-improvement 6. Ownership of work.

> Small changes: As mentioned previously, continuous improvement comes from many small changes rather than one large improvement. It is the sum of all these small steps that increases efficiency.

> Ideas from workers: In any business, a well trained workforce is its greatest asset. A worker may have hundreds of ideas about how to make their particular process more efficient. These ideas may be far more effective than if an external consultant or manager told them the best way to undertake a task. The challenge is to encourage these ideas and ensure they are acted upon.

> Spend small: Continuous improvement is not about buying one new piece of capital that will improve efficiency. Continuous improvements are likely going to cost nothing, or a small commitment to time and resources in printing a label or purchasing a new sign and some tape.

> Use your existing skill set: As mentioned earlier, a well trained workforce is a business's greatest asset. Use their skills. People have lives outside of work and many of these skills can be applied to the workforce. Ask a Gen Y to undertake a 5S audit and their first step may be to find a 5S template from an itunes app! The organisation may find these apps are the new standard work tool!

> Self-Improvement: It is important to develop a culture where employees are continually seeking ways to improve their own performance. Tools to help improve performance may be visual tools, or standard work charts so they understand what is important, and how to produce work efficiently. 6. Ownership of work: This is potentially the greatest change to continuous improvement. Staff need to feel they have both ownership and responsibility for their work. A culture of 'not my problem' is detrimental to continuous improvement. Staff taking ownership and responsibility will lead to some of the greatest improvements.

CONTINUOUS IMPROVEMENT IMPLEMENTATION

As can be seen, there are no hard or fast rules for continuous improvement. Continuous improvement is as much about a mindset change as it is about putting in place formal processes.

There are however some key techniques that wineries may wish to consider adopting, in order to implement CI practices into the business.

CONTINUOUS IMPROVEMENT BLITZ (KAIZEN BLITZ)

One technique to help kick start changes is a Continuous Improvement Blitz. This involves: 1. Training 2. Examining 3. Analyzing 4. Implementing 5. Checking and celebrating the change

This technique can be spaced over several days (or weeks) for a few hours each day. Ideally, this process should initially be implemented full time over one week to get the team moving to this culture change. It would be beneficial is this was repeated every few months until the culture becomes ingrained. These steps are explained in further detail below.

Training

The first step is to train the workforce. It is best at this time to give a broad overview of both lean management and tools available. This training is also the time to encourage a culture of 'no blame' and empowerment. Teams need to feel empowered to make decisions and contribute to their environment. It can start right from the training step. It is important that leaders attend these training sessions. All members of an organization need to contribute to continuous improvement and this needs to be demonstrated at the highest level – so training is the perfect opportunity. For the wine industry, training should ideally cover aspects of 5S Production, Standard Work, TPM, Visual Management, quick changeover and production leveling in the initial steps.

Examining

In the first instance, examination of workstations should be undertaken individually by operators. This provides a sense of ownership needed for continuous improvement. In subsequent blitzes, this may be done in groups to maximize the information and observations gained from the examination step. Photos of the current situation can help by providing information, and as a training exercise for 'before' and 'after' case studies.

Analyzing

Analyze the processes and look for efficiencies using lean tools and management. The opportunities may include things such as visual management implementation, 5S implementation, reducing movement, or reconfiguring workflows. It is important that this is discussed as a group activity. This allows brainstorming and provides new ideas. Remember, the key during this phase is encouraging everyone to participate, not just listening to the loudest talker. These people will be undertaking continuous improvement autonomously after the blitz.

Implementing

Implement the new practice making the process owner agrees with the changes. Hopefully the process owner has contributed to analyzing and coming up with solutions to their own workspace as this provides additional ownership and commitment. The changes, however, can be implemented by anyone – the importance here is to get the job done.

Checking and celebrating

This step allows the team to understand if the change is working or not. This involves looking at the process or workstation and checking how it is functioning. Using tools such as standardized work instruction sheet allows the processes efficiencies to be easily measured. Now it's time to celebrate the success of the project. Share the learnings of the process with all staff. Use photos to show staff the situation before and after implementation. It is only through this acknowledgement that continuous improvement will become a cultural change for the better.

APPLICATION IN THE WINE INDUSTRY

All tasks in the wine industry could benefit from continuous improvement. The key is encouraging this mindset. They are a few ways to kick start this process. Get your team together and ask them what works well in their area. More importantly, ask them what doesn't work well. Their responses can be primary targets for implementing continuous improvement blitz projects. Areas that deserve particular attention include receival to fermentation steps. In this case, it would involve getting a team together to observe the operation. During this observation, ask some of these questions: » How long does it take to empty a bin into the destemming hopper? » Where are grapes stored? » How far do the grapes need to travel to reach the hopper? » How many people are involved in the operation? » How many times does the operation stop and then start? » Is the hopper always full? » What are the bottlenecks? As can be seen in the above example, the situations and solutions are varied. All team members should have something to contribute to how processes can be run more efficiently. Once a new work flow, or process improvement has been established, it important to ensure staff don't go 'back to the old way'. Most of the time, staff will see and like the improvements, and these will remain the norm. If there is still resistance, it may be a sign that a part of the process is not working quite properly. Continuous Improvement has a great potential in reducing waste time, increasing staff morale, and increase staff ownership. Once the culture change has been implemented, it will reduce costs and benefit all members of the organization.

In conclusion, wines are alcoholic beverages that dates back in history and has been used for different purposes including religion and culinary purposes. There are different variants and classification of wine according to their color, taste, feel, fruit is it made from, terrior etc. wine makers are people who produce wines either for their business or employed by a wine making company and the process of wine making is known as vinification and it involves several stages. Viticulture is the process of growing grapes for wine production and it can be grown organically, conventionally or bio dynamically, depending on the wine makers preference. Natural wines are the ones that are made without major intervention during the winemaking process. Natural wines are not necessarily made from organic grapes, and at the same time organic wines are mostly about the grapes and not what happens in the winery. The latter process is exactly how you should differ these two kinds of wines - organic is about the grape, natural is about what happens at the winery. Lean Manufacturing is, therefore, all about the optimizing processes and eliminating waste. These seemingly simple efforts can greatly help with cutting costs while still delivering high-quality product customers want and are willing to pay for. The Lean approach is based on thoroughly evaluating your process to find what you're doing right and remove or adapt all steps that may be possibly generating waste. This waste is called muda and encompasses anything that doesn't add value to the end product. By adopting a lean philosophy, you enjoy the benefit of continuous improvement. It means that instead of making rapid, irregular and abrupt changes that are disruptive to the workplace, you'll make small and sustainable changes.

BIBLIOGRAPHY

- Jiménez, E., Tejeda, A. S., Pérez, M., Blanco, F., and Martínez. E. 2011, 'Applicability of lean production with VSM to the Rioja wine sector', *International Journal of Production Research, Taylor Francis*, pp.1. 10.1080/00207543.2011.561370. hal-00746093
- Swami, S. B. and Thakor, N. 2014, 'fruit wine production; a review', *Journal of Food Research and Technology*, Vol. 2, no. 3, pp. 93-100.

Learn

Catch up

A leader (or prince) might be a good person, but it's only essential for a prince to seem good to others

Don't be too generous, as it will only cause more greed

It is better to be feared than loved.

How to win friends and influence people- DC 1936

Be genuinely interested in other people

Smile

Be a good listener

Preparation

Don't fear the fear

Four Essential Elements of Your Personal Brand

1. Visibility
   Do people in your organization or community know who you are? Your presence felt by people you lead or the people want to lead? Findable where your desired networking contact are looking? Appear in the media, industry events, in the company cafeteria? Leaders need visibility.
2. Differentiation

What are you know for? What you can offer that other people can't? while leaders today need many skills, it can be helpful to have a few areas where you really excel. This is what gets you noticed and what gets you continually promoted.

3. Consistency

   Can people depend on you to behave in a similar way across a variety of circumstances? Treat people equally?

4. Authenticity

   Comfortable in your leadership skin? Maintain your personal integrity always.

What are you know for?

Ask people you trust. Ask a handful friends, mentors, colleagues, or family members to provide a few words to describe your professional skills and reputation. Be specific as possible.

Revisit recent reference letters, performance reviews, or other official documents in which someone has described you professionally.

Leader show commitment Act like a Leader

How to handle "you're Young Enough to Be my child"

Ignore it

Deflect it

Usually best option when someone treats you like a child in front of other people. Your goal with deflection is to appear polite but firm, and not to let the comment or action undermine your authority.

Confront it

If it happening over and over again with the same collegue or client. You might decide to address the situation directly.

Personal leadership Brand

A strong Self-introduction

A confident handshake

A level-up Wardrobe

Business Cards

Are going to be obsolete in a few years, today you still need them. Provide people with your contact information, so that what your cards should do. Now we have so many communication options, A business card can guide people to your preferred method, which is different for everyone these days. If you want people only to call your mobile phone, then only list the number on your card or list it before or above your landline. If you want people to email you instead of call to action on your card.

Lead

Listen: use the right method

Five essential rules as to communicate like a leader

Rule1. It's not about you

Rule2. Know your Audience

Rule3. Overcommunication Trumps Undercommunication

Rule4. Actually Listen

Start with Your Audience

Be open

Strive to Understand

Respond

Pause

Rule5: Your method matters

Choose right communication method

In person, Email , Phone, Voice Mail, Instant Message, Text

PS: Tell People the Best Way to communicate with you, too

Fourtheen Secrets of Great Communicators

1. They get the basics Right
2. They Eliminate Filler Words
3. They Avoid Upspeak
4. They Limit Cliches
5. They are concise
6. They show, Not tell
7. They Make Eye Contact
8. They Stand (and sit) Tall
9. They Don't Have All the Answers

    Refer, Defer, Infer

10. They are Discreet
11. They always have an ear to the Ground
12. They Face Conflict
13. They have a Sense of Humar
14. They Show Their passion

Become a Master of Meetings

Cancel it

Yep, you read that correctly. The first way to be a meeting master is to cancel as many meeting as possible. There is no rule saying you have to hold a certain meeting just because the previous boss always held that meeting. There is no law dictating that teams have to meet once a week whether there are issues to discuss or not. One of the first changes I made when I took over as board chair of she's First was to cancel all regular committee meetings until we determined which ones really needed to be held. Cancel any meeting that is not absolutely essential and you'll find that the meetings you do deem necessary are far more productive.

Keep it Small

Following the same principle, when you hold a meeting, invite the minimum number of participants possible.

Confirm

Send a shared calendar invitation or an email confirmation within twelve to twenty-four hours of meeting.

Set clear and realistic Agenda and stick to it

Start on time

 Keep up the energy

Stop the smartphones

Provide clear Next Steps

End Early

Change it Up

How to Give a Killer Presentation

Be smart about structure

Keep Time (Quietly)

You are the Presentation – Not Your Slides

Press " Record" Plan a great Ending

Manage

Three Essential Laws of 21st centry management

    1. Adaptability to Rapid Change: Technology, Employee Tenure, Time Lines

2. Cultural Awareness
3. Transparency

How to Manage People When you have zero experience Managing People

Be yourself

Launch a listening Tour

Drive the Truck

Secure Early Wins

Establish Key Performance Indicators

Managing is your job people I don't like.

Treat annoyer as your teacher

Shift your perspective

Focus on positives

How do I manage people don't seem to like me

Just as certain people will bug you, it's likely that you might bug other people. How do you deal with it when you sense someone on your team isn't a fan?

From Carol Frohlinger,

"First, I'd ask myself why. If it's one person that you feel doesn't like you, then that's one thing. If it's more than one, there may be a pattern that you might want to consider."

From Dr. Woody agrees

"Good management begins with introspection. You really have to understand how others react and respond to you, and you need to seek out that tough feedback from the people you manage directly and from colleagues. You have to constantly be willing to hear that feedback and adjust. We can come across differently than we think we do, and that could be harmful to build team cohesion."

Asking people "How am I doing?"

Just let them know that you are genuinely open to both positive and negative feedback and that there will be no backlash to any criticisms.

You don't have to accuse the other person of disliking you. Just ask for the feedback and listen with an open mind. You may receive some extremely helpful insight or you may even learn that the other person's dislike was all in your head.

How Do I confront Conflict

Since you can't avoid displeasing people sometimes, another reality of being a leader is that you'll have to become skilled at handling conflict.

Young leaders reprimand their employees by instant message, get into major strategy debates by text message, and even quit their job by email. More important issue is you will lose credibility quickly if you are unable to have difficult conversations in person or by phone.

Take your time

Bring solutions

Be a Broken Record

come up with your most important point or most compelling argument and repeat it no matter what counterargument the other person makes.

Bookend

Manaing your Mon or someone older

Don't assume Age is an Issue

Earn Respect by shown Respect

Motivation Nation: Eight ways to Inspire the Troops

1. Do the opposite of Every Bad Manager You've Ever Had
2. Manage by walking Around
3. Explain the Why
4. Show interest in Each Person's Self-development
5. Motivate Different Individuals in Different Ways
6. Encourage Excellece
7. Provide a safety Net
8. Change it Up

Ten Management Tips That Are Evergreen for a Reason

"Take one for the team"

"First in, Last Out"

"Hire People Smarter Than you Are"

"Practice What you Preach"

"Think Outside the Box"

"Do your Homework"

"It is What It is"

"It's Better to apologize Later Than ask Permission First"

"You have to pay your dues"

"Go the Extra Mile"

Prioritize

Busy is not a badge of Honor, and Five **More Time management Mantras**

Leadership is Marathon, Not a sprint

Take care of the big rocks First

An Ounce of Planning is worth a Pound of Work

Never Check E-mail in the morning

Stress is not actually coutagious

Handle Stress

Cut Down on decisions

Breath

Take Breaks

Connect

Strategies building relationships

1. Leave your Desk
2. Pick Up the Phone
   Leaving office and attending events helps you form relationships; the phone ensures you don't mess them up.
3. Build Relationship Before you need them
4. Give First
   "What can I do for you"
5. Ask, Too
   I admire the student who offered to help, and I also admire the CEO who admitted she needed help using her new phone. It's part of good relationship building to ask for assistance when you need it.
6. Always Take the meeting
7. Diversify
   If you only connected with people just like you, you wouldn't accomplish much (and you'd have a pretty boring life). Also challenge yourself to build relationships with people from other industries, countries, ethnicities, generations, regions, and political views. This may require stepping even further out of your comfort zone, and that's a good thing. Chat with peers in different department. Admin Assistants, baristas, temps, drivers. Leaders learn from everybody they meet.
8. Network Up

9. Take Notes
10. Follow up Faster

As a general rule, whenever you meet with someone for the first time, ask for someone's business card or contact info at a conference, or promise to provide somebody with followup information after a call or meeting, do it within twenty four hours. This sounds like a simple things, but I promise you will blow people away if you act this quickly. The world moves so fast these days that if you don't follow up with twenty four hrs, people basically moved on. "For every four business cards I give out, I get one follow-up." Be the one, and do it fast.

11. Know that Thank you is a Form of Networking

Networking, Six Online Tips
Do your Homework
Before reaching out or meeting with anyone, even someone you've met before, always google the person and thoroughly review his or her linkedin, recent tweets, and other social media profiles. Particularly important with new contacts.

"I was reading all about your recent ad campaign. I saw what your vcompetitors did and how you responded on your Twitter feed. I readlly admire how you handled it" Now you sound like a respectful collegue who is serious about building a relationship. That's who people want to know, net work with, and ultimately, do business with: people who do their homework.

Follow Organisations
Give people and Organizations Reasons to Reach out to You
Customize everything

Just because you can doesn't mean you should
Finally, remember that one of the benefits and dangers of social media is that it's easier than ever research other people, particular those with a relatively public persona.

Grow
Nine ways to get better all the Time
1. Trust your Training
2. Make yourself feel old

At the same time, you'll have to work hard to stay current. You'll be amazed at how fast the next generation sneaks up and you're the one complaining about kids today.

3. Stay Humble

There are times it will pay to be brash as a leader. There are infinitely more times it will pay to modest. Particularly if you're introverted by nature, do not feel the need to grow your head along with your career. In fact, you might be doing yourself disservice if you do so.

4. Decide to be Great

What makes a company- and a leader – become not just good but great?

People tend to respond by talking about the importance of hard work, which really is the price of admission to great leadership. When I pressed for my interviewees to tell me more ,to really explain what launches someone to the very elite level of his or her field, this is what many of them revealed to me : at a certain point as you are rising in your success, you need to *decide* to be the best. In other word, you can't just wait and hope that you rise to the top. You intentionally choose to go for it.

Can you really just decide to be a big success? I believe that if you make a definitive, no-turning-back-now choice to be the best and you couple that with hard, diligent work- and you do both hose things day in, day out, year in, year out, then, yes, there is no reason you can't achieve your biggest, boldest dreams.

5. Commit!

   While it's great to have options and be open to new opportunities, there comes a point where you have to start making some choices. If you want to be a great leader, you have to let the FOMO go. It will hold you back and frustrate the people around you. Take it from someone who has wasted way too much time and energy second – guessing decisions large and small.

6. Hatch some big idea

   When your mind is free of second-guessing past decisions and wondering about roads not taken, you'll have a lot more time and brain space to come up with the huge, innovative idea that can truly catapult your career.

7. Seek professional Help

8. Make your Own Rules

   All of the previous tips in this section make the assumption that you already know what your next leadership step is or what action would be require to get there. But, speaking as an entrepreneur, sometimes you have absolutely no idea what your next step will be because you're the very first person to forge your particular career path.

9. Change jobs

   No matter how happy you are in your current role or how much you are creating your own customized path, whether or not change your job will cross your mind at some point during your career. Should you start your own firm with some friends? Take a sabbatical to write a book? Jump to the competition?

   Some guideline

   More, pls: When to make a major move

   Some question to evaluating a major job move:

   Is it Truly an amazing opportunity?

   You may be content where you are, with coworkers you like, an important title, and work that meaningful. And then the phone rings and you receive an offer that's beyond anything you had ever imagined. Some opportunities have the potential to change your entire career – and life – trajectory.

   Eg, once you have the title of CEO on your resume or have launched a start-up that is acquired or goes public, you'll be playing in big leagues from that point forward.

   Are you following a trusted Mentor or Sponsor?

It's Flattering when your mentor asks you to come with her to her next gig, especially if it's high profile. But before you leap, ask yourself whether you are going because it's right move for you or because you feel like you can't say no to his particular person. You won't succeed if you're following some one else's dream, and your mentor, while disappointed, will untimately respect you for staying true to yourself.
Are you chasing a Dream?
Have you always imagined yourself building a business from ground up? Or does your childhood vision writing songs and singing them to sold out crowds keep rattling around in your brain? As long as you feel confident that you have a financial and personal plan for making your dream path a viable reality, then I would never stand in your way if the time feels right to leap toward your destiny.
Will you be making the world a better place?
If this is the type of move you want to make, then it can be a wise one.

In general, no guarantees that you are making the right decision. But as you'll see in the next section, every choice you make, even perceived career mistakes, will ultimately help you develop and grow.

How to fall with style
Own it -- How keep it short, be specific, Explain what you will do differently next time.
Lick your wounds. Privately
Don't make the same mistake Twice
Remember that Leadership is Hard
Never forget that by taking on a leadership role you have assumed a certain amount of risk. "With great power comes great responsibility" Leader ship will expose you to criticism, challenges, and annoyances large and small. And the more successful you become, the more impediments you are likely to face.
It helps in tough situation to remain focused on why you wanted to be a leader in the first place. "As long as you are motivated by a desire to make a positive impact, you cannot fail and will overcome the naysayers and the inevitable obstacles. You won't win every single battle, and there will be challenges. But every battle and every challenge is actually an opportunity – an opportunity to learn, to expand, to change course, to build character, and ultimately, to be a better servant leader."
Bounce Back Quickly
Share your lessons with others

Further Reading

Online sources

- https://en.m.wikipedia.org/wiki/Wine
- What is wine? | JancisRobinson.com
  https://www.jancisrobinson.com/learn/drinking-wine/what-is-wine

- 5 Stages of the Wine Making Process - Laurel Gray Vineyards
  http://laurelgray.com/5-stages-wine-making-process/
- 5 Reasons Why Great Wine Starts with Geography | Wine Folly
  https://www.google.com/amp/s/winefolly.com/tutorial/5-reasons-why-great-wine-starts-with-geography/
- Winery – Wikipedia
  https://en.m.wikipedia.org/wiki/Winery
- Storage - How Winemaking Works | HowStuffWorks
  https://science.howstuffworks.com/innovation/edible-innovations/winemaking5.htm
- Winemaking – Wikipedia
  https://en.m.wikipedia.org/wiki/Winemaking
- Fermentation and wine making
  http://www.morethanorganic.com/fermentation
- Why producers are turning to organic wine
  https://www.beveragedaily.com/Article/2018/02/06/Why-producers-are-turning-to-organic-wine
- Organic wine – Wikipedia
  https://en.m.wikipedia.org/wiki/Organic_wine
- What is Organic Wine? Biodynamic & Sulphite Free Wine Health Benefits - Organic Wine Club
  https://organicwineclub.co.uk/blogs/news/what-are-organic-wines-a-guide-on-organic-and-better-wines
- Biodynamic wine – Wikipedia
  https://en.m.wikipedia.org/wiki/Biodynamic_wine
- Introduction to Lean Manufacturing | Lean Production
  https://www.leanproduction.com/
- Top 25 Lean Manufacturing Tools | Lean Production
  https://www.leanproduction.com/top-25-lean-tools.html#25-essential-lean-tools
- What is lean manufacturing? | Basic concepts | Pipefy
  https://www.pipefy.com/blog/basic-concepts/what-is-lean-manufacturing/
- Lean manufacturing – Wikipedia
  https://en.m.wikipedia.org/wiki/Lean_manufacturing
- THE LEAN GUIDE: A PRIMER ON LEAN PRODUCTION FOR THE AUSTRALIAN WINE INDUSTRY https://www.wineaustralia.com/getmedia/b6b63b37-bde7-49ac-9e7f-b6a8d0fd44e2/2014_The-lean-guide.pdf

Lean

Lean thinking – banish waste and create wealth in your cooperation By James P. Womack and Daniel T. Jones

Lean supply chain management Essential- A framework for Material Managers. By Bill Kerber and B,J,Dreckshage.

Process Improvement and Design
Reengineering the corporation: A manifesto for businee revolution. By Hammer Michael and James champy. 1993
Managing Teams, By Holpp, Lawrence, 1999
Process innovation: reengineering Work through information Technology. By Davenport, Thomas H. 1993
Voice of Customer

How customer think: Essential Insights into the Mind of the Market by Gerald Zaltman
Learning and Innovation

The truth about Innovation By Max Mckeown

Leadership

Becoming the boss   By Lindsey Pollak

www.ingramcontent.com/pod-product-compliance
Lightning Source LLC
Chambersburg PA
CBHW061157180526
45170CB00002B/846